Shut Up, America!

Shut Up, America!

The End of Free Speech

by Brad O'Leary

WND BOOKS

SHUT UP, AMERICA! THE END OF FREE SPEECH
A WND Books book
Published by WorldNetDaily
Los Angeles, CA
Copyright © 2009 by Brad O'Leary

Cover image design: Mike Fitzgerald. Dust jacket design: Linda Daly.

WND Books are distributed to the trade by:
Midpoint Trade Books
27 West 20th Street, Suite 1102
New York, NY 10011

WND Books are available at special discounts for bulk purchases. WND Books, Inc. also publishes books in electronic formats. For more information call (310) 961–4170 or visit www.wndbooks.com.

First Edition

ISBN 13-Digit: 9781935071099
ISBN 10-Digit: 1935071092
E-Book ISBN 13-Digit: 9781935071631
E-Book ISBN 10-Digit: 1935071637
Library of Congress Control Number: 2009920919

Printed in the United States of America

10 9 8 7 6 5 4 3 2 1

This book is dedicated to my loving, caring and understanding wife,
who never tells me to "shut up."

Table of Contents

Introduction

"Restriction on free thought and free speech is the most dangerous of all subversions. It is the one un-American act that could most easily defeat us."

—U.S. Supreme Court Justice William O. Douglas

I N THE 2008 PRESIDENTIAL ELECTION, Congress issued no complaints about the content of television and print coverage of the race for the White House. But today's congressional leaders want to punish talk radio for its critical coverage of television and print media bias.

There is a core constituency in Congress that doesn't believe the free market of ideas, as top talk radio host Rush Limbaugh is fond of saying, is adequately serving the American people. This group believes it is the government's right to *force* an agenda onto the public, because the public is too unenlightened or too primitive or too provincial for its own good. In other words, this core constituency believes that you and I aren't smart enough to figure things out for ourselves, and that we need their help in order to form the correct points of view—*their* points of view. This group sees Americans as petulant children who refuse to eat their vegetables, and their solution is to forcefeed us what we clearly and definitively have rejected.

Moreover, this core constituency has found favor within the Democratic Party. And right now the Democratic majority in Congress, with help from the Obama administration, is plotting to reimpose the "Fairness Doctrine"—better named the "Censorship Doctrine"—and weaken the free exchange of ideas.

"It is incredible that in today's modern media age, where information is easily accessible in so many different forms, liberal Democrats want to squelch your First Amendment rights in favor of Chinese-style censorship," said Congressman Steve King (R-IA).[1]

King is right. If successful, these censorship advocates will destroy the central tenets of our way of life: freedom of thought, freedom of expression, and freedom to choose our own points of view.

Imagine an America where political speech over the airwaves is heavily regulated by government — regulated to the point of extinction. No more Rush Limbaugh. No more Sean Hannity. No more Glenn Beck. No more Laura Ingraham. No more counterbalance to the endless cadre of liberal foot soldiers who dominate network television, newspapers, and periodicals. No more free radio. And, for all intents and purposes, no more First Amendment.

As improbable as it sounds, for many of us it is not that hard to imagine, as this was America for nearly four dark decades.

Over 50 years ago, the Federal Communications Commission (FCC) enacted a draconian diktat with a most Orwellian name: the "Fairness Doctrine." This doctrine was to ensure that all so-called controversial issues addressed by broadcasters be *balanced and fair* — a standard that was decided arbitrarily by government officials.

In 1950 the FCC took the viewpoint that broadcast station licensees were "public trustees" and, as such, had an obligation "to afford reasonable opportunity for discussion of contrasting points of view on controversial issues of public importance."[2]

As if that were not enough, the Commission also held that stations were obligated to seek out issues that were important to their local communities, then air programming that addressed those "important" issues. Again, federal bureaucrats were the arbiters of what rose to the level of "importance."

What prompted government to execute such a Stalin-esque

takeover of the airwaves? According to the Museum of Broadcast Communications: "This doctrine grew out of concern that because of the large number of applications for radio stations being submitted and the limited number of frequencies available, broadcasters should make sure they did not use their stations simply as advocates with a singular perspective. Rather, they must allow all points of view."[3]

In other words, government was concerned that a single ideological force would gobble up all the available airspace and turn Americans into a bunch of monomaniacal knuckle-draggers. Government's solution was to assume quasi-fascist control of the airwaves, thereby ensuring the problem it set out to solve would be replaced by an even worse problem.

The Fairness Doctrine was anything but fair. Prior to the Fairness Doctrine, in the 1940s the FCC had established the "Mayflower Doctrine," which prohibited radio stations from editorializing. Thankfully, that absolute ban was vanquished in large part by the end of that decade, allowing editorializing so long as opposing points of view were permitted on the air. During those years, the FCC established *dicta* and case law which guided the operation of the agency's doctrine.[4]

The FCC later expanded upon what was considered acceptable and unacceptable speech and "editorializing."[5] By the early 1980s, however, the concept of the Fairness Doctrine was, not so ironically, deemed an impediment to the free flow of ideas, not a facilitator of them. American citizens, as well as the FCC itself, began to see it for what it really was: a *Censorship* Doctrine. In 1987, the FCC did away with the doctrine, ending government's stranglehold over the airwaves.

Of course the simple truth is that the doctrine was an impediment to freedom all along, not a guarantor of it. And this impediment served the liberal mainstream media elite well.

Whatever the FCC's intentions were, the application of the Fairness

Doctrine over the years became little more than an act whereby a gaggle of bureaucrats imposed *their* notion of "fairness" on the general public—without oversight or accountability. "Fair," simply defined, means "free from self-interest, prejudice, or favoritism." Yet by the very act of *imposing* fairness, those responsible act in their own self-interests and prejudices by showing favoritism for what they perceive to be a neglected ideal.

The idea that Americans should be forcefed content they don't want is the very antithesis of the principles of freedom our Founding Fathers fought and died to promote, protect, and preserve.

And what of the hapless owner of the broadcast medium? Should a privately owned company be forced to air content that alienates his core audience, thereby endangering the company's profitability and existence? The notion that the federal government can force the presentation of ideals—*any* ideals—on privately owned broadcast, print, or Internet-based businesses, at the risk of penalty or closure of those media businesses, is downright frightening. This is the same sort of iron-fisted censorship that Americans of all political persuasions decry when it rears its ugly head in countries like China, North Korea, and Cuba.

Can this really happen in *America*? Yes, as you will read in these pages. The votes currently exist in Congress to pass laws that censor talk radio. Obama stands poised to assemble a Federal Communications Commission that will seek to force radio station ownership changes and create rules to harass stations broadcasting views that counter those of the congressional leadership and the Obama administration.

Fortunately, conservative organizations and freedom-loving Americans everywhere are banding together to fight this attack on our First Amendment freedoms. But if we are to fight effectively, we must educate ourselves to the fullest extent possible. Fortunately,

Brad O'Leary has provided an excellent tool in this regard. If you cherish your First Amendment rights and want to preserve them, read this book and join the fight.

—**David Keene,** *President, American Conservative Union*

Chapter One

Left-wing Media Monopoly

"When I was a young reporter, I worked briefly for wire services, small radio stations, and newspapers, and I finally settled into a job at a large radio station owned by the Houston Chronicle. Almost immediately on starting work in that station's newsroom, I became aware of a concern which I had previously barely known existed—the FCC. The journalists at the Chronicle did not worry about it; those at the radio station did. Not only the station manager but the newspeople as well were very much aware of this government presence looking over their shoulders. I can recall newsroom conversations about what the FCC implications of broadcasting a particular report would be. Once a newsperson has to stop and consider what a government agency will think of something he or she wants to put on the air, an invaluable element of freedom has been lost."

—Former *CBS News* anchorman Dan Rather, in speaking out against the Fairness Doctrine in testimony to the Federal Communications Commission

WHEN IT COMES TO DEFINING the ideological slant of the mainstream media—generally considered to be the older television broadcast networks and major market newspapers—it is almost laughable to describe them as anything but left-wing or, at a minimum, left-of-center. Of course, the mainstream media mavens vehemently deny such accusations and do their best to turn attention away from their incredible bias and toward the supposed "bias" of their accusers.

However, the mainstream press's incessant fawning over Democratic presidential nominee Barack Obama in the 2008 campaign all but sealed the argument against the existence of institutional bias. Indeed, many media analysts point out that the coverage bordered on obsessive, with descriptions of Obama coverage ranging from overly complimentary to downright messianic.

Some longtime media professionals, in fact, were embarrassed.

"The sheer bias in the print and television coverage of [the 2008 presidential] election campaign is not just bewildering, but appalling," writes Michael S. Malone, a longtime journalist and author, in a column published by *ABC News Online* after the November 4, 2008 election. "And over the last few months I've found myself slowly moving from shaking my head at the obvious one-sided reporting, to actually shouting at the screen of my television and my laptop computer."[1]

Worst of all, Malone continues, "I've begun — for the first time in my adult life — to be embarrassed to admit what I do for a living. A few days ago, when asked by a new acquaintance what I did for a living, I replied that I was a 'writer,' because I couldn't bring myself to admit to a stranger that I'm a journalist."[2]

Deborah Howell, the ombudsman for the *Washington Post*, is much less critical but nevertheless finds a similar pro-Obama bias in her own newspaper.

"*The Post* provided a lot of good campaign coverage, but readers have been consistently critical of the lack of probing issues coverage and what they saw as a tilt toward Democrat Barack Obama. My surveys, which ended on Election Day, show that they are right on both counts," she writes in a November 9, 2008 column — again, *after* the election. "The count was lopsided, with 1,295 horse-race stories and 594 issues stories. *The Post* was deficient in stories that reported more than the two candidates trading jabs; readers needed articles, going back to the primaries, comparing their positions with outside experts' views. There were no broad stories on energy or science policy, and there were few on religion issues." She goes on to say, "The op-ed page ran far more laudatory opinion pieces on Obama, 32, than on [Republican presidential rival] Sen. John McCain, 13. There were far more negative pieces about McCain, 58, than there were about Obama, 32, and Obama got the editorial board's endorsement."[3]

Howell correctly lauds a sizeable portion of the paper's coverage as fair, but overall concludes: "Obama deserved tougher scrutiny than he got, especially of his undergraduate years, his start in Chicago and his relationship with Antoin "Tony" Rezko, who was convicted this year of influence-peddling in Chicago. *The Post* did nothing on Obama's acknowledged drug use as a teenager."[4]

As to the vice presidential candidates, Howell says of *The Post's* coverage, "One gaping hole in coverage involved [U.S. Sen.] Joe Biden [of Delaware], Obama's running mate. When Gov. Sarah Palin was nominated for vice president, reporters were booking the next flight to Alaska. Some readers thought *The Post* went over Palin with a fine-tooth comb and neglected Biden. They are right; it was a serious omission."[5]

Mark Halperin, of *Time* magazine and *ABC News*, called the lopsided coverage of Obama and his wife Michelle "disgusting," saying it desperately lacked any semblance of balance.

"It's the most disgusting failure of people in our business since the Iraq war," Halperin said at a post-election conference. "It was extreme bias, extreme pro-Obama coverage," he said.

"The example that I use, at the end of the campaign, was the two profiles that the *New York Times* ran of the potential first ladies," Halperin continued. "The story about Cindy McCain was vicious. It looked for every negative thing they could find about her and it cast her in an extraordinarily negative light. It didn't talk about her work, for instance, as a mother for her children, and they cherry-picked every negative thing that's ever been written about her." Michelle Obama's profile, however, was "like a front-page endorsement of what a great person Michelle Obama is."[6]

Jake Tapper, *ABC News* senior White House correspondent, agrees. He writes, in his online blog, that "perhaps the most unfair and negative TV ad run during the entire campaign, by either side, was the

Spanish-language TV ad Obama ran against [McCain] that got very little media coverage. Why didn't it get more coverage? If McCain had run a comparable ad—with unfair charges, trying to exploit racial tensions—would it have been as under-covered?"

"In any case," Tapper continues, "Obama won for any number of reasons, not the least of which were the modern Gold Standard in presidential campaigns and a nation that wanted a dramatic change. But I believe Halperin's larger point...the fact that reporters have an obligation to be better."[7]

An assessment of the problem was put very succinctly by Kevin Peters, a local news correspondent with KHOU-TV: "Studies show that Democrat Barack Obama gets more favorable coverage than Republican John McCain. In fact, a recent report from the Pew Research Center indicated that, on television and in newspapers, McCain endured twice as many negative stories as Obama."[8]

Interestingly enough, voters were already aware of the institutional liberal media bias during this election. Based on a Rasmussen Reports survey about the media's coverage of the 2008 election, just 17 percent of voters nationwide believed that most reporters tried to offer unbiased coverage, while the same survey found that nearly four times as many Americans—a whopping 68 percent—believed "most reporters try to help the candidate they want to win."[9]

Most Republicans and conservatives surveyed—82 percent—believe there was a bias in coverage, while far fewer Democrats and liberals (but still a majority at 56 percent) saw it. "Ideologically, political liberals give the least pessimistic assessment of reporters, but even 50 percent of those on the political left see bias," said the survey. "Among political conservatives, only 7 percent see reporters as objective while 83 percent believe they are biased."[10]

Concluded Rasmussen, "Given these results, it's not surprising that 76 percent of voters believe the media has too much power and influence over elections."[11]

Michael Malone says this about the problem:

> Now, of course, there's always been bias in the media. Human beings are biased, so the work they do, including reporting, is inevitably colored. Hell, I can show you 10 different ways to color variations of the word "said"—muttered, shouted, announced, reluctantly replied, responded, etc.—to influence the way a reader will comprehend exactly the same quote. We all learn that in Reporting 101, or at least in the first few weeks of working in a newsroom. But what we are also supposed to learn during that same apprenticeship is to recognize the dangerous power of that technique, and many others, and develop built-in alarms against them. But even more important, we are also supposed to be taught that even though there is no such thing as pure, Platonic objectivity in reporting, we are to spend our careers struggling to approach that ideal as closely as possible.[12]

In order to achieve that goal, reporters are supposed to be "constantly challenging our own prejudices, systematically presenting opposing views and never, ever burying stories that contradict our own world views or challenge people or institutions we admire," Malone writes. "If we can achieve Olympian detachment, then at least we can recognize human frailty—especially in ourselves," he says.[13]

As an example of institutional bias, Malone cites the mainstream media's treatment of the Palestinian-Israeli conflict. In that scenario, he says, Israel is portrayed so often as a mindless, crazed, bloodthirsty aggressor that finding objective coverage outside the Jewish state is nearly impossible.

As Israeli forces battled Iran-supported Hezbollah terrorists in the summer of 2005 in Lebanon, Malone sat in a hotel in Namibia watching the coverage on CNN International. He shouted at his TV as "one field reporter after another reported the carnage of the Israeli attacks in Beirut, with almost no corresponding coverage of the Hezbollah missiles raining down on northern Israel."[14]

The coverage "was so utterly and shamelessly biased," he says, "that I sat there for hours watching, assuming that eventually CNNi would get around to telling the rest of the story—but it never happened."[15]

Clearly, institutional media bias exists, especially when it comes to covering subjects and issues near and dear to the hearts of the mavens of the mainstream media.

Consider the case of Oprah Winfrey and her abysmal one-sided treatment of the presidential candidates during the 2008 election cycle. Granted, Oprah is not a traditional journalist but she certainly is a highly recognizable and influential media figure who commands a sizeable audience. As such, she could learn a lesson or two about checking her bias at the studio door, especially when millions of her viewers almost certainly do not share her liberal worldview.

Oprah, early on, endorsed Barack Obama. She hosted rallies and fundraisers for him that even he admitted gave him a boost.[16] She "used her program repeatedly to showcase, promote, and lionize" the eventual president-elect, said one analyst.[17] Following his Democratic National Convention speech at Invesco Field in Denver, Colorado, she publicly declared she had cried her "eyelashes off," that his words were "transcendent," and that the speech was "the most powerful thing I have ever experienced."[18]

On the other hand, Oprah steadfastly refused to interview GOP vice presidential contender and Alaska Governor Sarah Palin on her program before Election Day.

"At the beginning of the presidential campaign...I made the decision not to use my show as a platform for any of the candidates," she explained to *ABC News* in September 2008, after the story broke that she didn't want Palin on her show. That decision didn't stop her, however, from interviewing

Michelle Obama for the November issue of her magazine, O.

Palin's acceptance speech had attracted 37.2 million viewers—nearly as many as Obama's—and Oprah would have attracted millions of mostly female voters had she extended Palin the same courtesies that she extended to the Obamas.

"Oprah has worked hard to attract and hold the millions of viewers whose hypnotized eyes she sells to advertisers for astronomical profit," writes political analyst Lowell Ponte. "Leftists have rushed to her defense, chanting that Oprah has the right to interview whomever she wishes. These are the same leftists—lest we forget—who bray loudly for restoration of the...'Fairness Doctrine' to force left wing views onto talk radio stations regardless of owner or audience wishes. ... But when Oprah refuses to offer fairness and balance on her show, these same leftists stifle their mantras demanding 'fairness' on 'the public airwaves.' The double-standard hypocrisy of the Left and of Ms. Winfrey against fairness for Republicans is overwhelming."[19]

Even after Obama was elected, the mavens of the mainstream media continued to make no effort to hide their biased partisan preference for him:[20]

• During the Friday, November 21 evening news broadcast, all three major networks "touted how news that New York Federal Reserve President Tim Geithner will be nominated for Secretary of the Treasury fueled a [stock] market rebound" of about 300 points. What went unreported, however, was that earlier in the day, before the nomination, European stocks were already heading upward, as were U.S. stocks, on news that the federal government was extending financial bailout assistance worth tens of billions of dollars to troubled megabank Citigroup.

• The reactions of NBC's "journalists" were the most over-the-top, as an excited Andrea Mitchell lavished praise on President-elect Obama's "all-star cabinet" while gushing, "Obama is determined to pick the strongest, smartest people he can find, knowing that he is facing an economic crisis of historic proportions." A Nexis search, the Media Research Center (MRC) revealed, turned up no references on NBC, in the December 2000-January 2001 timeframe, to President-elect Bush's "all-star cabinet," even though he, too, chose "stars" like former Chairman of the Joint Chiefs of Staff Gen. Colin Powell.

• Appearing on the Friday, November 21, 2008 Today show, biased *Hardball* host Chris Matthews appeared more enthused about the incoming Obama administration than Obama's own spin doctors. Commenting on news that Democratic Sen. Hillary Clinton of New York, Obama's chief nomination rival, would accept a post as secretary of state in Obama's administration, Matthews called it "an astounding gesture of magnanimity." Matthews then swatted at the outgoing Bush administration, lecturing that the world is "waiting to see us back in that family of nations" and touted Bill Clinton's supposed popularity in global circles, according to MRC. Matthews even opined that despite past primary rivalries, the Hillary Clinton-Barack Obama "relationship is going by swimmingly."

• As noted by *Washington Post* ombudsman Deborah Howell, most of the mainstream media (to include her own newspaper) were far too lenient in their coverage and treatment of Obama. By comparison, the same mainstream mavens were ruthless to his opponents — even if, as in the case of Sen. Joe Lieberman (I-CT), they were fellow Democrats. (Lieberman lists himself as an "Independent;" however, he caucuses with Democrats in the Senate and derives his power and leadership posts from the Democratic Party). With "Any Regrets?" as the on-screen heading during her November 19, 2008 *CBS Evening News* broadcast, anchor Katie Couric pressed Lieberman to apologize for campaigning with GOP presidential candidate Sen. John McCain and criticizing eventual winner Barack Obama. Couric, in her first question, demanded to know, "Do you feel as if you owe President-elect Obama one?" She then pushed Lieberman to retract an observation he made:

"You said, on whether Senator Obama is a Marxist, you said quote: 'It's a good question to ask.' Are you sorry you said that?" She then proceeded to cast another Democratic aspersion on Lieberman: "What really irritated — even enraged — some Democrats was your speech at the Republican National

Convention. Did you understand at the time how nervy that might seem to some Democrats? How inappropriate?"

• At the top of the November 19, 2008 *CBS Early Show*, co-host Julie Chen proclaimed, "[I]t may be the hottest ticket in the country right now, a ticket to Barack Obama's inauguration in January. Millions are expected to try and watch the swearing in. But we're going to show you why tickets are almost impossible to get." But using the term millions was just a touch of an exaggeration. Chen later introduced a report on the Obama inauguration by proclaiming: "Inauguration fever is sweeping Washington. The city's mayor believes 3-5 million people may turn out to witness President-elect Obama's swearing-in." However, in the report, correspondent Thalia Assuras talked to Howard Gantman of the Joint Congressional Committee for Inauguration, who predicted a much smaller turnout: "We've printed 240,000 tickets. So that's a minimum, we expect at least that many people. For this event, we could see half a million, some projections have come in for a million or more."

Michael Malone points out that the country essentially elected "a cipher, who has left almost no paper trail, seems to have few friends (that at least will talk) and has entire years missing out of his biography." He correctly notes that "isn't...Obama's fault: His job [during the campaign] is to put his best face forward. No, it is the traditional media's fault, for it alone has had the resources to cover this story properly, and has systematically refused to do so."[21]

He notes that a lawyer for the McCain camp wondered aloud during the campaign why the country hadn't "seen an interview with Sen. Obama's grad school drug dealer—when we know all about Mrs. McCain's addiction [to Percocet and Vicodin]."[22] Malone also points out that interviews with Obama associate Bill Ayers, a co-founder of the 1960s-era terrorist Weather Underground group, and Tony Rezko, a Chicago developer convicted of political corruption, should have been pursued more fervently, but the mainstream media failed even to try.

Finally, Malone ponders why "[then-] Sen. Biden's endless gaffes almost [were] always covered up, or rationalized, by the traditional media?"[23]

Remember Joe "the Plumber" Wurzelbacher? He became famous overnight for asking Obama, while the presidential contender was campaigning in Wurzelbacher's Toledo, Ohio neighborhood, tough questions about his proposed plan to tax Americans earning more than $200,000. Though not everyone agreed with Wurzelbacher, tens of millions of Americans watched in disbelief as his life was torn asunder and uber-scrutinized by the mainstream media, all for asking questions *they* should have been asking.

It's clear that the media's bias has been evident for some time, but it is equally clear the bias reached new, epic proportions during the 2008 presidential campaign. For years, whistleblowers within the media establishment have sounded the alarm about it; before the 2008 election season a number of analysts predicted it; experts are now admitting it is rampant; the American public was witness to it; and most within the traditional, mainstream media are, as usual, denying it. Yet that same ideological bias that is so obvious in the traditional media currently has a stranglehold on Congress and the White House.

The mainstream media's track record on "fairness" is evident. We know what their definition of "fairness" is: "You can speak your mind as often and as loudly as you like — so long as you agree with us."

Freedom of speech, expression, and the press is not one-sided, but rather, ensures that a multitude of voices can be heard across different mediums. Were it not for talk radio during the 2008 presidential election, many would have known next to nothing about the real Barack Obama.

Chapter Two

The First Amendment Under Attack

"Whoever would overthrow the liberty of a nation must begin by subduing the freeness of speech."

—Benjamin Franklin

C ENSORSHIP HAS BEEN USED by kings and politicians to silence free speech since the ancient Greeks gave birth to democracy. Today, the ruling Democrats in Washington would like to eviscerate the First Amendment by enacting the "Fairness Doctrine," a more appropriate name for which would be the "Censorship Doctrine." The doctrine is specifically designed to legislate conservative talk radio out of business. Top-ranking Democrats in Congress have made no secret of their contempt for talk radio and their desire to kill it.

In an interview with *Fox News* in 2008, Sen. Charles Schumer (D-NY) compared conservative talk radio to "pornography,"[1] and said the Fairness Doctrine would only serve to make things more "fair and balanced."

In 2007, Senate Majority Whip Dick Durbin (D-IL) told *The Hill*: "It's time to reinstitute the Fairness Doctrine. I have this old-fashioned attitude that when Americans hear both sides of the story, they're in a better position to make a decision."[2]

Senate Rules Committee Chairwoman Dianne Feinstein (D-CA) wants to "look at the legal and constitutional aspects of" bringing back the Fairness Doctrine.[3]

"I believe very strongly that the airwaves are public and people use these airwaves for profit," she said. "But there is a responsibility to see that both sides and not just one side of the big public questions of the debate of the day are aired and are aired with some modicum of fairness."[4]

A recent Zogby poll showed that 53 percent of Americans who voted for Barack Obama would like to see the Fairness Doctrine resurrected, while only 37 percent would not (10 percent were undecided).

Left-wing think tanks like the George Soros-funded Center for American Progress have begun issuing studies and propaganda in support of enacting a new Fairness Doctrine.

Of course, none of these champions of censorship mentions the fact that the Left absolutely dominates nearly every other speech medium in America, including: movies, television (not only the big three networks, but cable as well), academia, newspapers, periodicals, so-called "public" radio and television, art, theatre, etc.

Talk radio is something left-wingers have not been able to make work for them, and what easier way to make it work than by legislative fiat in the form of censorship? They know that if they can censor talk radio, they can tighten their grip on power and better preserve their majority. To many of them, that would be well worth the price of a shredded First Amendment.

The People are Given the Power

Our Founding Fathers knew a thing or two about tyranny. After all, they risked much to sever from the overbearing reach of England. So it should be little surprise that their blueprint for American government is painstakingly and specifically designed to prevent that same tyranny from cropping up in the United States. With that in mind, it also makes perfect sense that the First Amendment to the U.S. Constitution—indeed, the very first guarantee in the Bill of Rights—is designed to protect free speech:

> Congress shall make no law respecting an establishment of religion, or prohibiting the free exercise thereof; or abridging the freedom of speech, or of the press; or the right of the people peaceably to assemble,

and to petition the Government for a redress of grievances.[5]

In just 45 words, our Founders clearly articulated their belief that real power should rest with the citizenry—not the government. They knew that the power to control the content of information, the spread of information, the freedom to form or join a group, and the freedom to believe or not believe as one chooses, is the power to oppress.

The First Amendment principally consists of five clauses that safeguard our freedom:

1. **The Establishment Clause** prevents government from adopting an official state religion.

2. **The Free Exercise Clause** guarantees that citizens may adhere to whatever religion they choose, and worship accordingly. This clause also protects our right to not adhere to any religion at all. All may believe or not believe as they choose.

3. **The Free Speech Clause** protects our God-given right to speak freely, even if what we say is controversial, offensive, or profane. This clause's protective umbrella extends beyond the mere spoken word—literary, commercial, and artistic speech are all covered.

4. **The Free Press Clause** protects our right to get information, unfettered and unfiltered, from a variety of sources: newspapers, radio, blogs, websites, television, magazines, e-mail, etc. In addition, this clause protects the freedom of the press itself and bars government from forcing people to publish what they don't want to publish, or withhold what they don't want to withhold.

5. **The Right to Assemble Clause** protects our right to join any group or organization for any reason. Groups can be religious, political, recreational, philanthropic, and, by definition, exclusionary. This clause also protects the rights of a group to exclude would-be members who don't fit the member-profile of the group.

Objectivity vs. Subjectivity in the Press

Before the advent of modern talk radio, the mainstream media (in particular, print media and major network television journalists) were considered beacons of objectivity by their loyal readers and viewers. It was believed that, when journalists received "professional training," they were taught to practice brutal objectivity when reporting "the news." Whatever biases or opinions they may have held were supposed to be checked at the door. They were, in essence, to behave similar to a judge on a bench — ignoring everything but the facts and reporting accordingly. This is the line we were sold, as we were conditioned to trust the media and view it as a purely objective and nearly robotic organ. Reporters gave us the news, and we formed our opinions.

The only problem with all of this was that it was completely untrue, and only over the last couple of decades have Americans truly begun to realize that the media emperor has no clothes when it comes to objectivity.

In fact, the mere act of reporting the news is inherently *subjective*. If you gave ten reporters a choice of three different breaking stories to cover, not all of them would pick the same story. Thus, before a journalist even puts ink to paper, or mouth to microphone, he or she has made a subjective decision.

Once a reporter decides to cover a story, more subjective decisions have to be made. Some facts are included while others are omitted. Objectivity isn't measured merely by what a journalist decides to say or write, but also by what he or she decides *not* to say or write. This is why assorted journalistic accounts of the exact same story all appear different. One version of a story might read: "Today, a dog jumped over a fire hydrant." Another might read: "Today, a dog jumped over a fire hydrant while being chased by a cat." And still another might read: "Today a dog jumped over a fire hydrant while being chased by a cat that the dog had bitten."

All of these accounts of the same story are true. All are factual. None overtly displays the opinion of the journalist. Yet, despite all of this, none of them can be said to be objective. And because they are subjective, they invoke different opinions. If you read only the first account, your opinion might be: "That's one lively dog." Readers of the second account might think: "That's one mean cat." And readers of the third account might think: "I hope that dog gets what it deserves."

Free Press = Free People

Journalistic "rules" and codes of conduct can't possibly guarantee thorough and accurate reporting—they never could and they never will. The only way to ensure that the truth, or as much of the truth as possible, makes its way to public ears and eyes is to protect the right of *all* media to investigate and report as they see fit across a wide array of mediums.

Declaration of Independence author Thomas Jefferson was keenly aware of this. Jefferson wrote to Judge John Tyler in 1804: "The firmness with which the people have withstood the abuses of the press, the discernment they have manifested between truth and falsehood, show that they may safely be trusted to hear everything true and false, and to form a correct judgment between them."[6]

The quintessential contemporary example of the timeless truth in Jefferson's words can be found in the infamous "Rathergate" incident. Veteran CBS anchorman Dan Rather, as you may know, is stalwart in his conviction that the "mainstream media" (of which he was once a chieftain) is without bias. In fact, he once said that liberal bias in the mainstream press was "one of the great political myths."[7] In his 1991 memoir, *I Remember*, he wrote: "My job is to be accurate and fair, an honest broker of information. Period." Notice the "period." He really believes that his reporting is the word and the truth, and should not be subject to any scrutiny by lesser beings. Of course, he isn't alone in this thinking. Most mainstream media bigwigs feel the same way.

It is fitting then that Dan Rather would make the ultimate case for why it is so critical to have multiple voices broadcasting freely across multiple mediums—and why entrusting a single body, or a "mainstream media," to be the sole arbiter of the news is extremely dangerous and destructive.

On September 8, 2004, Rather breathlessly reported on CBS's *60 Minutes* that he had obtained an election year bombshell. Rather displayed for the audience what appeared to be old Texas Air National Guard documents from the early '70s that showed President George W. Bush had shirked his National Guard duties. At least, that's what Rather believed, or wanted to believe, or wanted the American public to believe.

However, curious bloggers went to CBS's website to examine the supposedly damning documents. Within just 24 hours of Rather's story airing, it began to fall apart. These inquiring minds quickly discovered that the fonts and spaces used in the CBS documents were unlike any that could have been produced by a machine in the early 1970s. Therefore, the documents were modern day creations—forgeries.

Despite being obviously wrong, and despite the forgery story spreading like wildfire across talk radio and to every nook and cranny of the World Wide Web, CBS chose to take a slash-and-burn defensive posture. Rather tried to smear the bloggers as "partisan political operatives."[8] CBS's competitors closed ranks to protect one of their own. NBC anchorman Tom Brokaw guffawed that the bloggers were just on a "political jihad against Dan Rather and *CBS News* that is quite outrageous."[9]

Talk radio, on the other hand, beat the Rather story like a drum. Talk show hosts like Rush Limbaugh and Sean Hannity relentlessly reported about the bloggers' discovery of the phony documents. Now there was nowhere for CBS and Rather to hide. Virtually everyone in America knew the truth.

After being dragged kicking and screaming, CBS and Rather finally apologized to their viewers whom they had, either wittingly or unwittingly, duped. CBS was also forced to ax four senior executives involved with the story.

Now, what is really "quite outrageous" is the vitriolic indignation Brokaw and his "mainstream media" colleagues displayed over people investigating a story, discerning the truth, and correcting a lie. What is really "quite outrageous" is that a cooked-up story could have turned the tide of a presidential election.

Even more outrageous to think: Had CBS run a false story like that just a couple of decades earlier, it would have gone unnoticed and unchallenged. Lies would have been truth. There wouldn't have been bloggers to dig and sift and check the story's facts. And there wouldn't have been talk radio to take the facts and broadcast them over the airwaves.

The wrong reputations would have been ruined, and the ones that deserved ruining would have continued to glisten.

Thanks to freedom of the press, the freedom of bloggers and talk radio personalities to report and air whatever content they choose and as much of it as they choose—a colossal wrong was righted and minimal damage was done.

Regulations can't prevent the media from spreading lies, or ensure thorough, accurate, and balanced reporting. But a free press can.

The mainstream media's coverage of the 2008 presidential campaign was seen by many, including many within the mainstream media, as biased, if not fawning, for then-presidential candidate Barack Obama. This was true not only during the general election campaign but also during the primary season. Even *Saturday Night Live* spoofed the lopsided coverage the mainstream press gave to Obama over New York Sen. Hillary Clinton during their primary battle.

In November 2008, Zogby International conducted a post-election poll of Obama voters to gauge their knowledge of both the Obama/Biden and McCain/Palin tickets. The poll was commissioned by conservative talk show host John Ziegler, who wanted to determine what effect the mainstream media's lopsided coverage had on the electorate. The results were very interesting. According to a release on the poll results:

> Just 2% of voters who supported Barack Obama on Election Day obtained perfect or near-perfect scores on a post election test which gauged their knowledge of statements and scandals associated with the presidential tickets during the campaign, a new Zogby International telephone poll shows.

> Only 54% of Obama voters were able to answer at least half or more of the questions correctly.

> The 12-question, multiple-choice survey found questions regarding statements linked to Republican presidential candidate John McCain and his vice-presidential running-mate Sarah Palin were far more likely to be answered correctly by Obama voters than questions about statements associated with Obama and Vice-President–Elect Joe Biden. The telephone survey of 512 Obama voters nationwide was conducted Nov. 13-15, 2008, and carries a margin of error of +/- 4.4 percentage points…

> Ninety-four percent of Obama voters correctly identified Palin as the candidate with a pregnant teenage daughter, 86% correctly identified Palin as the candidate associated with a $150,000 wardrobe purchased by her political party, and 81% chose McCain as the candidate who was unable to identify the number of houses he owned. When asked which candidate said they could "see Russia from their house," 87% chose Palin, although the quote actually is attributed to Saturday Night Live's Tina Fey during her portrayal of Palin during the campaign. An answer of "none" or "Palin" was counted as a correct answer on the test, given that the statement was associated with a characterization of Palin.

> Obama voters did not fare nearly as well overall when asked to answer

questions about statements or stories associated with Obama or Biden—83% failed to correctly answer that Obama had won his first election by getting all of his opponents removed from the ballot, and 88% did not correctly associate Obama with his statement that his energy policies would likely bankrupt the coal industry. Most (56%) were also not able to correctly answer that Obama started his political career at the home of two former members of the Weather Underground.

Nearly three quarters (72%) of Obama voters did not correctly identify Biden as the candidate who had to quit a previous campaign for President because he was found to have plagiarized a speech, and nearly half (47%) did not know that Biden was the one who predicted Obama would be tested by a generated international crisis during his first six months as President.

In addition to questions regarding statements and scandals associated with the campaigns, the 12-question, multiple-choice survey also included a question asking which political party controlled both houses of Congress leading up to the election—57% of Obama voters were unable to correctly answer that Democrats controlled both the House and the Senate.[10]

Considering how uninformed, and even misinformed, much of the American electorate seems to be, we need more free, unencumbered voices—not fewer.

No Free Press = Oppressed People

Every year, the nonprofit, free press group, Reporters Without Borders, releases a World Press Freedom Index which ranks nations top to bottom in terms of press freedom. Most won't be surprised to find that the most tyrannical nations on earth ranked at the bottom of the Press Freedom Index in 2008. Somalia, Afghanistan, Syria, Libya, Iran, China, Cuba, and North Korea were all in the bottom 20 (out of 173 nations ranked).[11] The United States came in at number 36. The top ten includes countries like Iceland, Norway, Finland, Ireland, and Sweden.

Why do tyrannical nations run by despots, dictators, and severely oppressive ruling parties not have a free press? Is this coincidence? Hardly.

The best way for an oppressive dictator or party to maintain its power is to make certain that its opinion or point of view is the only one its citizens ever hear. In short, if you can control the content and spread of information you can control the citizenry.

Take, for instance, the Xinhua News Agency. A state-run media organ of the Chinese government, Xinhua's job is to report—or, more accurately, to *manufacture*—the news. At the same time, China also employs an army of media cops to monitor websites and blogs for any content that does not toe its communist party line.

Reporters Without Borders calls Xinhua "the world's biggest propaganda agency."[12] According to the group:

> Despite a certain economic liberalisation of the media sector, Xinhua remains the voice of the sole party. Hand-picked journalists, who are regularly indoctrinated, produce reports for the Chinese media that give the official point of view and others - classified "internal reference" for the country's leaders.

> After being criticised for its lack of transparency, particularly during the Sars epidemic, Xinhua has for last few months been putting out news reports embarrassing to the government, but they are designed to fool the international community, since they are not published in Chinese.[13]

This frightening brand of state information manipulation is straight out of George Orwell's epic novel *1984*.

It should be noted that China adopted, or rather issued, a state constitution in 1982, dubbed "The Constitution of the People's Republic of China." The clear purpose of this document, however, is not to guarantee basic rights and freedoms to Chinese citizens. Rather, the objective of the Chinese constitution is to give the *impression* to Chinese citizens, and the international community, that freedom and individual liberty are alive and well in China.

For instance, here is what the Chinese constitution says about freedom of the press: "Citizens of the People's Republic of China enjoy freedom of speech, of the press, of assembly, of association, of procession and of demonstration."[14]

Nowhere in this article is the freedom of speech or press specifically guaranteed. Rather, the article reads more like a public relations statement, and a dishonest one at that. Just ask the untold numbers of media who have been detained or executed for exercising their "freedom of press." Exercising free speech, or simply reporting and publishing truths that might be inconvenient to the objectives of the ruling party in China, is akin to suicide. China and Cuba have the notorious distinction of being the two biggest prisons for journalists.[15]

The relationship between the freedom of speech and press, and the freedom of the people, is clear. Neither can exist without the other. A tyrannical government with the power to control speech and information is exactly what our Founders sought to prevent when they gave us the Bill of Rights over two centuries ago.

Chapter Three

History of Suppression

"Reactionary liberalism, the ideology of many Democrats, holds that inconvenient rights such as secret ballots in unionization elections should be repealed; that existing failures such as GM should be preserved; and, with special perversity, that repealed mistakes such as the 'fairness doctrine' should be repeated. That Orwellian name was designed to disguise the doctrine's use as the government's instrument for preventing fair competition in the broadcasting of political commentary.

Because liberals have been even less successful in competing with conservatives on talk radio than Detroit has been in competing with its rivals, liberals are seeking protectionism in the form of regulations that suppress rivals."

— **Nationally Syndicated Columnist George Will**

T ODAY'S CONSERVATIVE TALK RADIO was born at KFBK radio in Sacramento, California, when in 1987, a young Rush Limbaugh set fire to the airwaves. Of course, KFBK had actually hired Limbaugh in 1984. However, it wasn't until 1987, when President Ronald Reagan's Federal Communications Commission lifted the censorship shackles of the so-called Fairness Doctrine and restored Limbaugh's, and every other broadcaster's and station owner's right to free speech.

Limbaugh was finally free to speak his mind to a hungry audience and his career took off, paving the way for today's 2,000 voices of freedom on the airwaves.

Without question, the Fairness Doctrine, when it was still in effect, was not a means to guarantee equity of viewpoints, but rather a policy that inhibited the free airing and exchange of ideas enshrined in the very First Amendment to the U.S. Constitution. It was censorship, plain and simple.

Even if the government's initial intent had been to create an environment offering equal time to all points of view, the doctrine strayed so far from that ideal that it was derided as the "Unfairness Doctrine" by many of its critics.

Such critics included even liberal bastions like the *Washington Post* and the *New York Times*. In a 1987 editorial, the *Post* called the Fairness Doctrine "dangerous," "repulsive," and a threat to democracy:

> "The truth is...that there is no 'fairness' whatever in the 'fairness' doctrine. On the contrary, it is a chilling federal attempt to compel some undefined 'balance' of what ideas radio and television news programs are to include.... The 'fairness doctrine' undercuts free, independent, sound and responsive journalism—substituting governmental dictates. That is deceptive, dangerous and, in a democracy, repulsive."[1]

When it was implemented by the Federal Communications Commission in 1949, the intent of the doctrine was to require broadcasters to "afford reasonable opportunity for the discussion of conflicting views of public importance."[2]

At the time broadcasters—who were then and still are licensed by the Commission—were considered by the government to be "public trustees" of the airwaves (or, really, employees of the government) and, as such, "had an obligation to afford reasonable opportunity for discussion of contrasting points of view [as determined by the FCC] on controversial issues of public importance."[3]

The FCC was concerned that the large number of applications for radio stations would outpace the limited number of frequencies available. Thus, the thinking went, it might have been too easy for a relative few who did get licenses to use their stations to advocate a single point of view. The FCC wanted to make certain that no such monopoly of the airwaves occurred.[4]

By the 1950s and 1960s, the FCC had become much more involved in defining what its commissioners believed was "editorializing" and a lack of balance in broadcasting. In 1967, for example, the FCC laid out rules which defined such matters as "personal attack and political editorializing."[5] Four years later, in 1971, the Commission "set requirements for the stations to report, with their license renewal, efforts to seek out and address issues of concern to the community."[6] This reporting requirement became known as "Ascertainment of Community Needs," and was to be done systematically by station management personnel. Now, new attempts are being made to bring this back and drastically shorten the station license renewal period from the current eight-year term to two years. And enemies of free speech want to have every station subject to a local community board so liberal activists in San Francisco, New York, Boston, or wherever, can decide if Limbaugh, Hannity, Levin, and Gallagher represent the views of the greater community, and thus, whether or not their programs should continue to air.

The Fairness Doctrine ran parallel to another federal law, passed in 1937, known as the "Communications Act." Section 315 of the Act required stations to offer "equal opportunity" to all legally qualified political candidates for any office, if that station had allowed anyone running for that office to use the station. Section 315 exempted news programs, interviews and documentaries but the FCC-imposed Fairness Doctrine covered those efforts. The other major difference between the two regulatory efforts was that the Communications Act was federal law, whereas the FCC's Fairness Doctrine was merely departmental policy.

The doctrine remained simply a matter of general policy and was applied on a case-by-case basis until 1967. When certain provisions of the doctrine were incorporated as FCC regulations, they did not require equal time for opposing views but instead required that opposing views be presented. Stations were given latitude on how they could present contrasting views: they could be presented through news segments, public affairs shows, or editorials.

In 1969 the doctrine was given much credence in the U.S. Supreme Court case, *Red Lion Broadcasting Co., Inc. v. FCC*:

> In that case, a station in Pennsylvania, licensed by Red Lion Co., had aired a "Christian Crusade" program wherein an author, Fred J. Cook, was attacked. When Cook requested time to reply in keeping with the fairness doctrine, the station refused. Upon appeal to the FCC, the Commission declared that there was personal attack and the station had failed to meet its obligation. The station appealed and the case wended its way through the courts and eventually to the Supreme Court. The court ruled for the FCC, giving sanction to the fairness doctrine.[7]

In its decision, the high court ruled that the doctrine did not violate a broadcaster's First Amendment rights:

> A license permits broadcasting, but the licensee has no constitutional right to be the one who holds the license or to monopolize a...frequency to the exclusion of his fellow citizens. There is nothing in the First Amendment which prevents the Government from requiring a licensee to share his frequency with others.... It is the right of the viewers and listeners, not the right of the broadcasters, which is paramount.[8]

Still, the court cautioned "that if the doctrine ever began to restrain speech, then the rule's constitutionality should be reconsidered."[9]

Seemingly, the court recognized the serious flaws of the doctrine, and may have known then that it was only a matter of time before the doctrine would full reveal itself as a tool for censorship.

Just five years later, the high court ruled—without declaring the policy unconstitutional—that it "inescapably dampens the vigor and limits the variety of public debate (*Miami Herald Publishing Co.*

v. Tornillo, 418 U.S. 241)."[10]

A decade later, in 1984, the high court again considered a case born out of frustration and resentment over the Fairness Doctrine. In that case (*FCC v. League of Women Voters*, 468 U.S. 364) a majority of high court justices "concluded that the scarcity rationale underlying the doctrine was flawed and that the doctrine was limiting the breadth of public debate."[11]

In that case, the court's very close 5-4 majority decision by Justice William J. Brennan, Jr., stated that, while many then considered that expanding sources of communication made the doctrine's limits unnecessary, "we are not prepared, however, to reconsider our longstanding approach without some signal from Congress or the FCC that technological developments have advanced so far that some revision of the system of broadcast regulation may be required."

After noting that the FCC was considering repealing the Fairness Doctrine rules on editorials and personal attacks out of fear that those rules might be "chilling speech," the high court added:

> Of course, the Commission may, in the exercise of its discretion, decide to modify or abandon these rules, and we express no view on the legality of either course. As we recognized in Red Lion, however, were it to be shown by the Commission that the fairness doctrine "[has] the net effect of reducing rather than enhancing" speech, we would then be forced to reconsider the constitutional basis of our decision in that case.[12]

Death of Censorship

Even before the doctrine's demise, it was getting low marks from print and television journalists who were bothered by the high court's initial decision in the Red Lion case. Rightfully so, they considered the policy a gross violation of the First Amendment's Freedom of Speech and

Freedom of the Press provisions, which protect the right of writers and broadcasters to make their own decisions about balancing stories. But to comply with the mandate to provide contrasting points of view, reporters and journalists simply avoided any coverage of issues that could be considered even remotely controversial. The end result was not a freer exchange of ideas and *more* balance, but a less free exchange and *less* balance—just the opposite of what the FCC was trying to achieve.

Also, by the late 1970s and early 1980s broadcast journalism had changed and expanded dramatically. The "scarcity" and "public trustee" arguments that drove the government to implement the Fairness Doctrine were fast disappearing. Thousands of radio stations were springing up across the land, and the birth of cable television meant there were scores more channels to watch.

By 1985 the FCC, under Chairman Mark S. Fowler, a communications attorney who had served on Ronald Reagan's presidential campaign staff in 1976 and 1980, began to dismantle parts of the doctrine. The Commission noted that the doctrine hurt the public interest and was in violation of the First Amendment's Free Speech Clause.

In one landmark case, the FCC argued that *teletext*, a new technology by which text could be transmitted via television, created soaring demand for a limited resource and thus could be exempt from the Fairness Doctrine. The Telecommunications Research and Action Center (TRAC) and Media Access Project (MAP) argued that teletext transmissions should be regulated like any other airwave technology, hence the Fairness Doctrine was applicable (and must be enforced by the FCC).

In 1986 U.S. District Judge Robert Bork and his colleague, Antonin Scalia—both of whom sat on the U.S. District Court of Appeals for the District of Columbia - concluded that the Fairness Doctrine could apply to teletext, but that the FCC was not required to apply it.[13] This ruling proved to be a critical blow. The following year, in *Meredith Corp. v. FCC*, two other judges on the same court declared that because Congress did not mandate the doctrine in the first place, the FCC did not have to continue to enforce it.[14]

In August 1987, the FCC abolished the doctrine by a 4-0 vote, in the *Syracuse Peace Council* decision, which was upheld by a different panel of the Appeals Court for the D.C. Circuit in February 1989. The FCC stated, "the intrusion by government into the content of programming occasioned by the enforcement of [the Fairness Doctrine] restricts the journalistic freedom of broadcasters...[and] actually inhibits the presentation of controversial issues of public importance to the detriment of the public and the degradation of the editorial prerogative of broadcast journalists," and suggested that, because of the many media voices in the marketplace, the doctrine be deemed unconstitutional.[15] Frighteningly, this vote to abolish the Fairness Doctrine was made possible only when then-FCC chairman and censorship proponent Henry Rivera stepped down and was replaced by free speech advocate Patricia Diaz Dennis.

In its *League of Women Voters* ruling, the high court acknowledged that "the broadcasting industry operates under restrictions not imposed on other media." As such, though the "thrust" of the doctrine's restrictions "has generally been to secure the public's First Amendment interest in receiving a balanced presentation of view on diverse matters of public concern," the result was that "the absolute freedom to advocate one's own positions without also presenting opposing viewpoints—a freedom enjoyed, for example, by newspaper publishers—is denied to broadcasters."[16]

Now it was clear. The doctrine had stripped broadcasters of their free speech rights.

Fowler, during his tenure at FCC chairman, held the same point of view.

"Fowler said he wanted to go beyond mere negative burden lifting to bring a bold new principle to communications policy: broadcasting, he proclaimed, should receive the same First Amendment protection as the print media have always enjoyed," Henry Geller, the former general counsel of the FCC, wrote in the March/April 1983 issue of *Regulation* magazine.[17]

Undaunted by the realization that the doctrine was unfair, unconstitutional, and ineffective—and aware that successive high court decisions were paving the way to a repeal of bad policy—champions of government control nevertheless tried to have it enshrined as the law of the land, not simply a policy the FCC was to enforce.

In the spring of 1987 both Houses of Congress voted to put the Fairness Doctrine into law, but President Reagan vetoed the measure, and there were insufficient votes to override his veto. Essentially, Reagan kept his oath to uphold the Constitution, even if some in Congress were willing to violate theirs.

Foes of free speech and open debate tried once more during the administration of Reagan's successor George H.W. Bush, but they failed again when Bush vetoed that legislation.

But let it be clear: Both times Congress had the votes to censor radio, so it should be no surprise that, in 2009 and beyond, Congress will have the votes once again to impose censorship. However, this time they will have a president whose party leaders and supporters are in favor of such an action. Undoubtedly, the president himself will support it as well.

Two lingering rules of the doctrine—the "personal attack" rule and the "political editorial" rule—managed to survive until 2000. The personal attack rule was applied whenever a person or small group became subjected to a personal attack during a broadcast. In that event, stations had to notify the persons or group within a week, provide them a full transcript of what was said, and offer them the opportunity to respond on-air. The political editorial rule applied when a station broadcast editorials endorsing or opposing candidates for public office. It required that the unendorsed candidates be notified, then allowed a reasonable chance at rebuttal.

In light of its decision to repeal the Fairness Doctrine, the U.S. Court of Appeals for the D.C. Circuit ordered the FCC to justify these rules. Then in 2000, when the agency did not provide prompt justification, the court ordered their repeal.

And good riddance. After all, what other journalistic mediums, such as print or television, are required to give equal time to anyone they criticize? Imagine if the *New York Times* had to abide by such a law? Republicans and conservatives would have full-time jobs writing daily rebuttals.

Faulty premise

When commercial broadcasting was in its infancy and few stations were on the air, the worry that a station owner could monopolize a particular point of view might have been a legitimate concern. But once it became evident that both radio and television broadcasting were expanding at a brisk pace, the idea that the government should continue regulating speech became ludicrous. At that point its interference became that of a censor, not a force for "fairness." But today's new breed of Fairness Doctrine advocates is still clinging to this faulty and outdated logic.

"Supporters of the fairness doctrine argue that because the airwaves are a scarce resource, they should be policed by federal bureaucrats to ensure that all viewpoints are heard. Yet, just because the spectrum within which broadcast frequencies are found has boundaries, it does not mean that there is a practical shortage of views being heard over the airwaves," writes Adam Thierer, in a paper for the Heritage Foundation. "When the fairness doctrine was first conceived, only 2,881 radio and

98 television stations existed. By 1960, there were 4,309 radio and 569 television stations. By 1989, these numbers grew to over 10,000 radio stations and close to 1,400 television stations."[18]

Today, there are there are 4,776 AM stations, 6,309 FMs, and 2,892 educational FMs, which the FCC lists separately.[19] Those figures don't include an additional 831 low-power FM stations.[20]

What is probably the most egregious of all claims by advocates of a government-enforced censorship doctrine is that they believe only a federal bureaucracy can accurately define and mete out "fairness." But the fact is FCC bureaucrats—or those from any similar agency acting in a similar capacity—don't have the *capability* to be fair. The way the system is set up essentially negates an environment of fairness. An FCC bureaucrat's idea of fairness would invariably rest on how *he* defined it and, since such posts are politically appointed, who can seriously say a political appointee will be *fair* to a broadcaster who is making his living airing content critical of the current, appointing, administration?

Such institutional unfairness has happened before. Telecommunications scholar Thomas W. Hazlett noted that under the Republican administration of President Richard M. Nixon, "License harassment of stations considered unfriendly to the administration became a regular time on the agenda at White House policy meetings."[21]

Finally, those who advocate for a return of the doctrine still argue that it will enhance, not limit, debate. But the truth, in the words of Adam Thierer, is that "arbitrary enforcement of the fairness doctrine will diminish rigorous debate."[22]

"[W]ith the threat of potential FCC retaliation for perceived lack of compliance, most broadcasters would be more reluctant to air their own opinions because it might require them to air alternative perspectives that their audience does not want to hear," Thierer says. "Thus, the result of the fairness doctrine in many cases would be to stifle the growth of disseminating views and, in effect, make free speech less."[23]

Such institutional abuse of the doctrine has been bipartisan. Bill Ruder, a former official in the Democratic administration of President John F. Kennedy, said, "We had a massive strategy to use the fairness doctrine to challenge and harass the right-wing broadcasters, and hope the challenge would be so costly to them that they would be inhibited and decide it was too expensive to continue."[24]

During the 2008 presidential campaign, the Obama camp tried to bully Chicago radio station WGN-AM into barring writers and Obama critics, David Freddoso and Stanley Kurtz, from receiving any airtime. The Obama team recruited over 100,000 activists to besiege the station, in a cult-like fashion, with phone calls and e-mails. Imagine if Obama had the power of the Fairness Doctrine.

"The fairness doctrine remains just beneath the surface of concerns over broadcasting and cablecasting, and some members of Congress continue to threaten to pass it into legislation," wrote Val E. Limberg, of the Museum of Broadcast Communications—in the mid-1990s, *more than 10 years ago.*

Indeed, censorship proponents have never had a riper environment in Congress and the White House to resurrect the Fairness Doctrine and bury free speech than they have today. What was once a threat may soon become reality.

Chapter Four

Targeting Free Speech

"The framers of the First Amendment, confident that public debate would be freer and healthier without the kind of interference represented by the 'Fairness Doctrine,' chose to forbid such regulations in the clearest terms: 'Congress shall make no law...abridging the freedom of speech, or of the press.'"

—President Ronald Reagan in 1987, when vetoing a bill that would have enshrined the Fairness Doctrine in U.S. law

"EVERYONE RECOGNIZES TODAY we are in the midst of a media revolution. But has anyone considered when that revolution began?"[1]

That's the way Joseph Farah, founder and editor-in-chief of *WorldNetDaily.com*, begins his July 31, 2007 column. In answering his own question, Farah puts the date at August 4, 1987, the date the FCC abolished the Fairness Doctrine.

It was on that day, he says, "something momentous," "something wonderful," and "something that changed the world for the better" happened.[2] With the demise of the Fairness Doctrine, he argues, freedom and open, lively political debate began in earnest.

At the time, Farah points out, there were just three major broadcast networks, each of whose nightly newscasts featured "semi-official" content that was "remarkably similar" to the others, "almost as if they were produced by the same team."[3]

In fact, he says, they were: by the editorial staff of the *New York Times*. Much of the Big Three networks' content, Farah writes, came from the Gray Lady herself. And, because of the *Times'* politically skewed coverage, many of the day's important issues were presented only from a slanted, one-sided point of view.

Also, at that time there were only 75 radio talk shows in the entire country.[4] *Only 75.* By comparison, today there are over 3,000 — two-thirds of which offer "countless points of view from the extreme left to the extreme right and everything in between"[5]).

Also, in 1987 there was no Internet or, at least, no widespread use of the Internet Americans currently enjoy. So, consequently, there were no 'New Media' voices — web-based news sites, blogs, alternative webzines, etc. — to offer competing points of view.

In short, there was a dearth of debate and no free exchange of ideas. All of that changed, however, after President Ronald Reagan stopped short a congressional effort to enshrine into law the most blatant attack on the First Amendment ever devised.

But unfortunately, Reagan's veto pen didn't settle the issue for good. In fact, thanks to their regaining the White House in 2008 and keeping control over both Houses of Congress, Democrats on the far left are poised to reintroduce a modern-day censorship version of the Fairness Doctrine that will eventually encompass more than just talk radio, although that medium is most certainly the likely first target of today's newest assault on free speech.

The threat to reimpose the Fairness Doctrine has been well documented. A number of Democratic Party members and their leaders in Congress have made numerous statements about bringing it back and making it law, rather than just a regulatory policy within the scope of the FCC.

"For many, many years we operated under a Fairness Doctrine in this country," Sen. Jeff Bingaman (D-NM) told Newsradio KKOB, in Albuquerque. "I would want this station and all stations to have to present a balanced perspective and different points of view, instead of always hammering away at one side of the political [spectrum]."[6]

The Hill, Congress' daily newspaper, quoted Sen. Charles Schumer (D-NY) as saying he was all for re-implementation of the Fairness Doctrine. In fact, he compares political speech to pornography.

"Asked if he is a supporter of telling radio stations what content they should have, Schumer uses the fair and balanced line, claiming that critics of the Fairness Doctrine are being inconsistent," the paper reported regarding an interview Schumer did on Fox News—ironically enough on Election Day '08. "I think we should all be fair and balanced, don't you? ... The very same people who don't want the Fairness Doctrine want the FCC [Federal Communications Commission] to limit pornography on the air," ...says Schumer.[7]

Senate Rules Committee Chairwoman Sen. Dianne Feinstein agrees. She said, in 2007, "I believe very strongly that the airwaves are public and people use these airwaves for profit. But there is a responsibility to see that both sides and not just one side of the big public questions of debate of the day are aired and are aired with some modicum of fairness."[8] She went onto say, "In my view, talk radio tends to be one-sided. It also tends to be dwelling in hyperbole. It's explosive. It pushes people to, I think, extreme views without a lot of information.... I'm looking at [the Fairness Doctrine].... Unfortunately, talk radio is overwhelmingly one way."[9]

Sen. John Kerry, the Democratic Party's 2004 nominee, also supports a new Fairness Doctrine. In a radio interview with Brian Lehrer on WNYC in New York City, Kerry directly tied reimposing the doctrine specifically as a way to drown out *conservative* voices on the airwaves. Broadcasting & Cable reported on Kerry's interview:

Calling it one of the "most profound changes in the balance of the media," he said conservatives have been able to "squeeze down and squeeze out opinion of opposing views. I think it has been a very important transition in the imbalance of our public dialog."

"I think the Fairness Doctrine ought to be there, and I also think equal time doctrine ought to come back," Kerry complained.[11]

During a May 30, 2007 interview with CBS morning host Harry Smith, former Vice President-et-savior of the earth, Al Gore, bashed Reagan's decision to veto legislation to bring back the Fairness Doctrine, claiming it was an assault on "democracy":

> [T]he first concerns among defenders of democracy arose with radio. And that's why the equal time provision and the Fairness Doctrine and the public interest standard were put in place here. Those protections were almost completely removed during President Reagan's term.[12]

Despite denials, clearly there is an effort underway by Democrats to reinstate the doctrine, and the intent is to put a muzzle on any dissention. Officially, as candidate Obama, the president said he wouldn't seek to reimpose it. But clearly his party's elders — Pelosi, Kerry, Boxer, Feinstein, Schumer, and Durbin — want it, and badly. They see it as their best hedge against any ideas that compete with their own. Rep. Anna Eshoo (D–CA), who sits on the House Energy and Commerce Committee chaired by fellow California Democrat Henry Waxman, pledged to work to bring the Fairness Doctrine back and make it apply to cable and satellite television as well as broadcast radio and network television.

Calling All Censors

In June 2007, the House of Representatives voted overwhelmingly (309-115) "to prohibit the Federal Communications Commission (FCC) from using taxpayer dollars to impose the Fairness Doctrine on broadcasters who feature conservative radio hosts such as Rush Limbaugh and Sean Hannity," *The Hill* reported.[13]

By a large margin "lawmakers amended the Financial Services and General Government appropriations bill to bar the FCC from requiring broadcasters to balance conservative content with liberal programming such as Air America," the congressional newspaper said.[14]

The legislation was co-sponsored by a conservative Republican and former talk radio host, Rep. Mike Pence of Indiana, because he wanted to force the issue and put Democrats and opponents of free speech on record.

"This House will say what some in the other body are not saying, that we believe in freedom on the airwaves," Pence said of the Senate. "We reject the doctrines of the past that would have this federal government manage political speech on the public airwaves."[15]

Rep. Jeff Flake (R-AZ), a co-sponsor of the legislation, lauded its failure, saying, "Rather than having the government regulate what people can say, we should let the market decide what people want to hear. That's precisely why the Fairness Doctrine was abandoned, and that's why it ought not to be revived."[16]

House Minority Leader John Boehner (R-OH) said listeners themselves were best suited to decide on what content and point of view they wanted to hear. "The best way is to let the judgment of the American people decide, and they can decide with their finger," he said. "[People] can turn it off or they can turn it on. They can go to their computer and read it on the Internet."[17]

Some Democrats who voted with Republicans sought to downplay the significance of the messengers, not the message.

"We ought to let right-wing talk radio go on as they do now," said Democratic House Appropriations Committee Chairman David Obey of Wisconsin. "Rush [Limbaugh] and Sean [Hannity] are just about as important in the scheme of things as Paris Hilton, and I would hate to see them gain an ounce of credibility by being forced by a government agency or anybody else to moderate their views enough that they might become modestly influential or respected."[18]

Attempts to ridicule today's top talkers notwithstanding, the effort to silence them nonetheless will continue unabated, simply because there are too many leftist censorship advocates in Congress who believe squelching debate is the only way to get the American people to buy what they're selling.

Pending legislation

What form might a new Fairness Doctrine take? Would it encompass only radio broadcasting or would it be expanded to cover political speech on television, on the Internet, and in political magazines? There is a recent legislative model on which to base a number of presumptions about what direction the Stalin-esque effort to reinstate the Fairness Doctrine might take in the very near future.

The Media Ownership Reform Act, or MORA, originally introduced in the spring of 2004 by Rep. Maurice Hinchey (D-NY), "included regulations that would prohibit consolidation and mass domination of broadcasting groups to serve the public interest," as well as a new Fairness Doctrine.[19] Hinchey also tried to get MORA passed in February 2007. That quiet, second attempt failed, but the bill remains.

According to media expert Adam Thierer, who has closely examined the measure, the Hinchey bill proposes a "radical re-regulation of the media marketplace in America." It "would not only undo all the limited ownership reforms that the FCC pushed through last summer, it would reinstate cable–broadcaster cross-ownership regulations that were struck down by the courts and more tightly restrict the number of radio stations a firm can own locally and nationally." Finally, "the bill would resurrect two disastrous FCC rules that were thought to have been swept into the dustbin of history long ago: the so-called 'Fin-Syn' rules and the hideously misnamed Fairness Doctrine."[20]

Thierer describes Fin-Syn:[21]

The Financial Interest and Syndication (or "Fin-Syn") rules were put into effect by the FCC in 1970 to prohibit a TV network from holding a financial stake in independently produced programs. Networks were forced to either purchase all of their programming from independent producers or develop programs in-house. But in-house production capabilities were also limited by consent decrees that the three major television networks were forced to enter with the Justice Department. The logic behind these restrictions was that vertical integration of broadcast television program creation and distribution would allow broadcasters to gain excessive control over prime-time programming on their airwaves. But by 1993, the FCC came to realize that the Fin-Syn rules were counterproductive and began dismantling them. The result was a great deregulatory success story. In the wake of decontrol, media operators were free to structure new business arrangements and alliances to finance increasingly expensive new programs, as well as entirely new networks and cable stations. (The UPN and WB television networks largely owe their existence to the repeal of Fin-Syn.) Also, by eliminating Fin-Syn and allowing greater integration of programming and distribution, content providers were able to ensure that their shows were given wider distribution on not only network television but cable channels as well.

Critics of abolishing the Fin-Syn requirements made the same disproven arguments that backers of the Fairness Doctrine have always made: that removing the requirements would discourage "alternative voices" on the airwaves and, hence, limit debate.[22]

In fact, the measure's intent—to stifle the free flow of ideas rather than promote them—is stated clearly in the bill's summary: "To amend the Communications Act of 1934 to prevent excessive concentration of ownership of the nation's media outlets, *to restore fairness in broadcasting, and to foster and promote localism, diversity, and competition in the media"* (my emphasis).

Plus, as many opponents of the Hinchey measure point out, while it criticizes and proposes to re-regulate broadcast media, there is no similar language to apply the Fairness Doctrine to newspapers, Internet-based publications, and other forms of political speech. Part of that could be that the bill's supporters will handle those mediums in separate legislation, as many opponents of the doctrine fear. But part of it could also be that so much of traditional media—especially newspapers, for instance—are already in ideological lockstep with the very same censors seeking to muzzle their competition, most of which comes from the booming talk radio industry.

Still, Fairness Doctrinaires eventually will have to impose their mandates on other mediums because, by any measure, circulation and advertising figures for the country's major traditional newspapers are rapidly declining.

"For the reporting period ending September 30, 2007, the *Atlanta Journal-Constitution* was down 8.9 percent daily and 9.2 percent Sunday; the *San Diego Union-Tribune*, 8.2 percent daily and 7.9 percent Sunday; the *Dallas Morning News*, 8.0 percent daily and 7.6 percent Sunday; and the *Boston Globe*, 6.6 percent daily and 6.5 percent Sunday. All were engaged in some of the voluntary trimming of distribution to distant areas," said a Project for Excellence in Journalism "State of the News Media 2008" annual report on American journalism.[23] In that same report, the study showed that circulation for "The Old Gray Lady," the *New York Times*, fell 4.6 percent daily and 7.6 percent for Sunday.[24]

The liberals' once-dominant media forum is fading fast, in part because Americans have discovered real diversity of ideas elsewhere. The enemies of free speech know this. They also know that, if they are to accomplish their goal of stifling all debate, they will have to control *all* media outlets.

In one final attempt to regulate content, the Hinchey bill's strict new ownership limits on radio, television, cable, and satellite broadcasters account only for *channels* or *frequencies* owned, not for format. The bill makes no distinction, for example, between AM and FM frequencies on the radio dial; or whether a cable broadcaster owns a shopping channel, an outdoors channel, a news channel, or a channel that features dancing polar bears. Restrictions imposed by the bill are much stricter than those which currently exist.

Under MORA, a broadcast radio company could own only a certain number of stations in a geographic region, serving a set number of people. The bill makes no distinction between the kinds of content aired on each of the stations owned by the broadcaster. Moreover, if a broadcaster owned more stations in a region than MORA allowed, the company would be *required* "to divest itself of such licenses as may be necessary to come into compliance with such limitation within one year after the date of enactment."[25] In other words, if a broadcaster owned more stations than allowed by MORA, the company would have to give them up (along with the profits each station was generating). Also, under MORA it makes no difference if the broadcaster owns talk radio stations airing political or issue-oriented speech, or stations broadcasting country music, classic rock, or sports.

The same principle applies to cable and satellite broadcasters. As for syndicators, the rules appear vague, but it is only a matter of time before the enemies of free speech extend their reach to a syndication company featuring content with one primary political point of view.

Preempting lost freedom

Just as there is a legislative effort to reinstate the Fairness Doctrine, there is also one to permanently prevent it from ever again becoming reality.

Backers of the First Amendment have introduced the "Broadcaster Freedom Act" which would permanently ban the doctrine. Although the new, larger Democratic House majority may not allow it to see the light of day, the summary of this one-page bill reads simply, "To prevent the Federal Communications Commission from repromulgating the Fairness Doctrine."

According to the Act's sponsor, Rep. Mike Pence:

> Bringing back the Fairness Doctrine would amount to government control over political views expressed on the public airwaves. It is a dangerous proposal to suggest the government should be in the business of rationing free speech...

> The Broadcaster Freedom Act will prohibit the Federal Communications Commission from prescribing rules, regulations, or policies that will reinstate the requirement that broadcasters present opposing viewpoints in controversial issues of public importance. The Broadcaster Freedom Act will prevent the FCC or any future President from reinstating the Fairness Doctrine. This legislation ensures true freedom and fairness will remain on our radio airwaves, and I would encourage my colleagues to cosponsor and support this bill.[26]

Pence's effort may be too little, too late, especially considering the results of the 2008 elections. Not only did a left-wing Democrat win the White House—the *National Journal* rated him the *most* liberal U.S. senator in 2007—but dozens of like-minded Democratic allies also won seats, as the party extended its previous majority.

Congressman Peter King (R-NY) has introduced the Free Speech Protection Act, a much-needed bill that does seem to have broad support (Senators Lieberman and Schumer have co-sponsored a companion bill in the Senate). The Act would protect American citizens from foreign libel judgments if their actions would not be considered libel under U.S.

law.[27] The legislation is modeled after a similar bill that passed in New York, dubbed "Rachel's Law."

Rachel Ehrenfeld is an American scholar, author, and internationally respected authority on the subject of terror finance. She holds a Ph.D. in criminology from Hebrew University School of Law and has testified in her area of expertise before both the U.S. Congress and the European Parliament.

In her best seller, *Funding Evil: How Terrorism is Financed and How to Stop It* (Bonus Books, 2003, 2005) Dr. Ehrenfeld identified Khalid bin Mahfouz, banker to the Saudi royal family and one of the world's richest men, as a leading terrorism financier. Bin Mahfouz sued Ehrenfeld for libel in British court (a practice known as "libel tourism") on the grounds that a small number of books had been sold and shipped to Britons. Because British libel law is extremely liberal and often used successfully to squelch free speech, bin Mahfouz won his suit and an award of $225,000.[28]

Ehrenfeld sought protection in the New York court system, but the courts couldn't assert jurisdiction over bin Mahfouz. At that point the New York State Legislature sprang into action and quickly passed the Libel Terrorism Protection Act, also known as "Rachel's Law", which "grants New York courts jurisdiction over persons who obtain foreign libel judgments against New York writers or publishers and limits enforcement of foreign libel judgments to those rendered under legal systems that meet the standards of the U.S. First Amendment."[29]

The King bill is very important, as many nations don't have the same strong free speech protections that the U.S. guarantees in the First Amendment. The United Nations, for its part, is also trying to clamp down on free speech by criminalizing any form of speech that can be loosely considered defamatory toward a religion. In November 2008, The UN General Assembly's Third Committee passed the "Combating

Defamation of Religions" resolution which would do exactly that.[30] The measure was sponsored by the Organization of the Islamic Conference as a way to criminalize any criticism of Islam. As of this writing, the resolution has not received a final vote.[31]

As for President Obama, he certainly has telegraphed his intentions. During the 2008 presidential campaign, he displayed an iron-fisted intolerance for free speech and freedom of the press.

For example, when Texan Harold Simmons ran a TV ad questioning Obama's association with former FBI "most wanted" and communist Bill Ayers, Obama went so far as to ask the Justice Department to investigate any TV station that ran the ad.

In Missouri, the Obama campaign assembled a so-called "truth squad," comprised of members of the local law enforcement community. The squad's purpose was to target and intimidate any media outlets that reported any disparaging news about Obama.[32]

And perhaps most telling of all, soon after he was elected Obama appointed former FCC Commissioner and Fairness Doctrine proponent Henry Rivera to head his FCC transition team. Rivera served on the five-member FCC board from 1981 to 1985. In 1986, President Reagan replaced Rivera with Patricia Diaz Dennis—a free speech advocate and opponent of the Fairness Doctrine. Dennis's appointment led to the repeal of the doctrine in 1987.

When news of Obama's Rivera appointment broke, free speech and free press advocates rang the alarm bells. The blogosphere and talk radio relentlessly pursued the story and informed the American public all about Rivera's history of promoting censorship. As a result, Rivera enjoyed his new post as FCC transition leader for only about a week before the Obama camp reassigned him to a transition team focused on science and technology. The official explanation for Rivera's reassignment was that his lobbying and legal work on communications issues ran afoul of conflict-of-interest rules. However, the immediate and loud outcry over Rivera's appointment, and the swiftness with which he was relocated, signify that his departure from the FCC transition post was as much a political damage control move as it was an effort to comply with rules.

Obama's Democratic colleagues in Congress have also made known their animus for conservative talk radio.

In the fall of 2007, Senate Majority Leader Harry Reid (D-NV), along with 40 other Democratic members of the Senate lambasted top talker Rush Limbaugh, demanding he apologize for something he never even said. Senators who signed the letter were: Harry Reid, Richard Durbin, Charles Schumer, Patty Murray, Daniel Akaka, Max Baucus, Joseph Biden, Barbara Boxer, Sherrod Brown, Robert Byrd, Benjamin Cardin, Tom Carper, Bob Casey, Hillary Rodham Clinton, Kent Conrad, Christopher Dodd, Byron Dorgan, Dianne Feinstein, Tom Harkin, Daniel Inouye, Edward M. Kennedy, John Kerry, Amy Klobuchar, Mary Landrieu, Frank Lautenberg, Patrick Leahy, Carl Levin, Blanche Lincoln, Bob Menendez, Barbara Mikulski, Bill Nelson, Barack Obama, Jack Reed, Jay Rockefeller, Ken Salazar, Bernie Sanders, Debbie Stabenow, Jon Tester, Jim Webb, Sheldon Whitehouse, and Ron Wyden.

Reid made the following statement on the floor of the U.S. Senate October 1, 2007, regarding Rush's alleged comments:

Freedom of speech is one of our country's most cherished values. Nothing sets us further apart from the countries and regimes we oppose than our belief that everyone's opinion matters, and everyone has the right to express it. That is why, when we hear things on the radio that are offensive, by and large, we tolerate them.

But last week, Rush Limbaugh went way over the line—and while we respect his right to say anything he likes, his unpatriotic comments cannot be ignored. During his show last Wednesday, Rush Limbaugh was engaged in one of his typical rants. This rant was unremarkable and indistinguishable from his usual drivel, which has been steadily losing listeners for years — until he crossed that line by calling our men and women in uniform who oppose the war in Iraq 'phony soldiers.' This comment was so beyond the pale of decency that it cannot be left alone. And yet, he followed it up with denials and an attack on Congressman Jack Murtha, a 37-year active member of the Marine Corps... Rush Limbaugh took it upon himself to attack the courage and character of those fighting and dying for him and for all of us.[33]

Reid's own rant came on top of a letter he and the 40 other members signed to Mark Mays, the chief executive of Clear Channel, who syndicates Limbaugh's program:

Although Americans of goodwill debate the merits of this war, we can all agree that those who serve with such great courage deserve our deepest respect and gratitude. That is why Rush Limbaugh's recent characterization of troops who oppose the war as "phony soldiers" is such an outrage. Our troops are fighting and dying to bring to others the freedoms that many take for granted. It is unconscionable that Mr. Limbaugh would criticize them for exercising the fundamentally American right to free speech. Mr. Limbaugh has made outrageous remarks before, but this affront to our soldiers is beyond the pale... Thousands of active troops and veterans were subjected to Mr. Limbaugh's unpatriotic and indefensible comments on your broadcast. We trust you will agree that not a single one of our sons, daughters, neighbors and friends serving overseas is a 'phony soldier.' We call on you to publicly repudiate these comments that call into question their service and sacrifice and to ask Mr. Limbaugh to apologize for his comments.

Here is what Limbaugh *really* said, as he explained on his daily program September 28, 2007:

I call this the anatomy of a smear, and what this is, is a great illustration of the liberals and the Democrat Party playbook for '08, which is underway now. The morning update on Wednesday dealt with a soldier, a fake, phony soldier by the name of Jesse MacBeth who never served in Iraq; he was never an Army Ranger. He was drummed out of the military in 44 days. He had his day in court; he never got the Purple Heart as he claimed, and he described all these war atrocities. He became a hero to the anti-war left. They love phony soldiers, and they prop 'em up. When it is demonstrated that they have been lying about things, then they just forget about it. There's no retraction; there's no apology; there's no, "Uh-oh, sorry." After doing that morning update on Wednesday, I got a phone call yesterday from somebody, we were talking about the troops, and this gentleman said something which you'll hear here in just a second, prompting me to reply "yeah, the phony soldiers."[34]

Limbaugh went on to explain—and his on-air show archives corroborate—that he wasn't talking about American troops in general, but instead the *one soldier*—MacBeth—who claimed to have attained the rank of corporal, claimed to have earned a purple heart for sustaining wounds in battle, claimed to be an elite Army Ranger, and claimed to witness U.S. troops committing horrors in Iraq.

"We would burn their bodies. We would hang their bodies from the rafters in the mosque," MacBeth described, in actions he and other soldiers allegedly took against suspected militants overseas.

But, as Limbaugh pointed out, none of what MacBeth claimed was true, as a military court would later discover:

Now, recently, Jesse MacBeth, poster boy for the anti-war left, had his day in court. And you know what? He was sentenced to five months in jail and three years probation for falsifying a Department of Veterans Affairs claim and his Army discharge record. He was in the Army. Jesse MacBeth was in the Army, folks, briefly. Forty-four days before he washed out of boot camp. Jesse MacBeth isn't an Army Ranger, never

47

was. He isn't a corporal, never was. He never won the Purple Heart, and he was never in combat to witness the horrors he claimed to have seen.[35]

Limbaugh went on to point out that "not one member of the media, not one congressman, nobody…called our office to ask, 'Did you really say this? And what did you mean by it?'"

Rather, he said, they *chose* to take his comments out of context, both to serve a political agenda and, more importantly some believe, to remind Limbaugh and others who ideologically oppose Reid and Co. that *they*, not the Limbaughs of the world, have ultimate control over their broadcast destinies. Reid made it clear that only U.S. senators should be granted the right to lie — which is their spin on the right to free speech.

The Reid-sponsored letter "was a brazen power play," says Joseph Farah. It "was a shot across the bow by an arrogant group of petty, wannabe tyrants who would, if they could, use the coercive power of the state to stifle all dissenting views."[37]

He's right. They seek to use the power of the state, in Orwellian fashion, to control speech, not to protect it or foster it. By any definition, that is censorship.

In his classic thriller, "1984," author George Orwell vividly describes the totalitarian mindset and demonstrates how tyrants can make words mean the exact opposite of their true definitions. "Black was white. Peace became war. Truth became lie."[38] Moreover, Orwell based his book on a real-life modern-day example of totalitarianism: the former Soviet Union.

According to an ATI-News/Zogby poll conducted in October 2008 — less than a week before the November 4, 2008 election — "Obama backers are at odds even with independents and undecided voters on the issue of clamping down on free speech on the airwaves."[39]

The survey found that those who said they were likely to support Obama for president "supported reinstating the 'Fairness Doctrine' by a margin of 49 percent to 36 percent, and Democrats support it 47 [percent] to 38 percent," said the report.[40]

"But then the poll asked, 'Some say the Fairness Doctrine could result in popular radio shows, such as Sean Hannity or Rush Limbaugh, to be taken off the air in some markets. Knowing this, do you support or oppose reinstatement of the Fairness Doctrine?" the report said.[41]

The results were disturbing. Those who said they would vote for Obama supported reinstating the doctrine 53-37 percent—even as independent voters opposed the doctrine 49-40 percent, and undecided voters rejected its reinstatement 50-17 percent.

The results showed that Obama's supporters would rather silence their detractors through censorship than compete ideologically with opponents.

Regulatory push

There is other evidence that reintroduction of the Fairness Doctrine could be just around the corner.

In June 2008, House Minority Leader John Boehner (R-OH) charged in a public letter to then-FCC Chairman Kevin J. Martin that his agency was seeking to secretly reinstate the doctrine, despite the agency's denial.

"Under the rubric of 'broadcast localism' it is clear the Commission is proposing no less than a sweeping takeover by Washington bureaucrats of broadcast media," Boehner wrote. "The proposals and recommendations for Commission action contained in the Notice of Proposed Rulemaking amount to the stealth enactment of the Fairness Doctrine, a policy designated to squelch the free speech and free expression of specifically targeted audiences."[43]

Boehner's letter was accompanied by a press release, which noted, "The rules, proposed by the FCC earlier this year, would reinstitute advisory boards to regulate broadcast content and revive a host of other rules the Commission dropped more than 20 years ago."[44]

Writing in a commentary for the Free Congress Foundation, the late Paul M. Weyrich said sources at the FCC insisted the rulemaking process was "in no way a back door to the Fairness Doctrine." Rather, "it is simply an attempt to get at big companies that are not fulfilling their requirements to the public in order to have their free license to use the public airwaves. There are localism requirements to use the public airwaves just as there are indecency rules. You have to have some relationship with the area in which you are licensed to serve."[45]

Boehner argued the so-called "advisory boards" were of a bygone era and would actually saddle broadcast media with onerous bureaucratic burdens not similarly faced by cable and satellite broadcasters or the Internet. And Weyrich further noted that the FCC report's assertion that the boards would help radio stations "determine the needs and interests of their communities" or "promote localism and diversity" borders on fantasy.[46]

Some believe Senate Majority Leader Harry Reid, with the help of fellow Democrats, could seek to stack the FCC with like-minded members, thereby setting up reinstatement of the doctrine by default—now that his chamber, like the House, expanded its majority in the 2008 elections.

Thankfully, not everyone in Congress shares the notion that the government should be regulating speech.

"The American people love a fair fight and so do I, especially where the issues of the day are debated," Rep. Pence writes in an editorial in *Human Events* magazine. "In a free market, fairness should be determined based upon equal opportunity, not equal results. Some voices are calling for Congress to enforce their idea of 'fairness' on our broadcast airwaves.

But our nation should proceed with caution whenever some would achieve their 'fairness' by limiting the freedom of others."[47]

One of the Democrats' most championed heroes is President John F. Kennedy, whose administration was anything but tolerant of opposing viewpoints. But in a moment of brutal honesty, even he acknowledged that freedom can be advanced through a diversity of ideas:

> We are not afraid to entrust the American people with unpleasant facts, foreign ideas, alien philosophies, and competitive values. For a nation that is afraid to let its people judge the truth and falsehood in an open market is a nation that is afraid of its people.

Chapter Five
The Incumbent Protection Act

"Conservatives, historically uninterested in mobilizing against 'reform,' have tended to depend on the courts to strike down the worst laws. Indeed, many believe that President Bush signed McCain-Feingold because his legal advisers assured him that the courts would never tolerate the law's new restrictions. But the Supreme Court has been erratic in protecting political speech. In McConnell v. FEC, the case that upheld McCain-Feingold, the Court gave political speech less protection than Internet pornography, simulated child pornography, topless dancing, tobacco advertising, and the dissemination of illegally acquired information."

—Bradley A. Smith, Law Professor and Former Chairman of the Federal Election Commission

(AUTHOR'S NOTE: This chapter is a warning to anyone who thinks that the federal courts will protect free speech in spite of what Congress or the FCC decides on the Fairness Doctrine.)

P OWER, IN ITS PUREST, most corrupting form, is the driving force behind politicians' desire to clamp down on free speech and regulate the press. Since the dawn of time, rulers (or, more accurately, despots) have sought to control the information available to citizens as a way of keeping citizens complacent, and thus, assuring their own grip on power.

In this context, the free speech-killing "Bipartisan Campaign Reform Act of 2002" (also named "McCain-Feingold," after its two main authors, Sens. John McCain (R-AZ) and Russell Feingold (D-WI), makes perfect sense. However, that such a law could be passed by 240 members of the U.S. House and 60 members of the U.S. Senate, and be signed by President George W. Bush—all of whom swore an oath to support and defend the U.S. Constitution (First Amendment included) — makes zero sense.

Even the title of the bill is grossly misleading, as Democrats in both the House and Senate provided the overwhelming majority of support and votes for the supposedly "bipartisan" Act. In reality, 79 percent of Republicans in the House voted against the measure, as did 78 percent of Republicans in the Senate.

Opponents of McCain-Feingold have rightfully dubbed the bill "The Incumbent Protection Act," as that is what it is specifically designed to do: make it as difficult as possible for an office-seeking challenger to dethrone a sitting representative or senator. Champions of McCain-Feingold argued for the measure under the guise of safeguarding elections from corruption. As columnist George Will writes:

> Congress is less divided by partisanship than it is united by devotion to the practice of protecting incumbents…The law's ostensible purpose is to combat corruption or the appearance thereof. But by restricting the quantity and regulating the content and timing of political speech, the law serves incumbents, who are better known than most challengers, more able to raise money and uniquely able to use aspects of their offices — franked mail, legislative initiatives, C-SPAN, news conferences — for self-promotion.[1]

CATO Institute president Ed Crane strikes a similar chord in describing the unfair, and blatantly unconstitutional, advantage McCain-Feingold gives incumbents. Says Crane:

> There is not a line in McCain-Feingold that isn't designed to protect incumbents. The so-called Bipartisan Campaign Reform Act makes it a crime to even mention the name of a candidate for federal office in a radio or television ad within 60 days of a general election. No criticizing incumbents!… Incumbents have earmarks to pass around and large mailing lists. Challengers do not. Advantage, incumbents.[2]

The degree to which the legislation stifles political speech is downright frightening.

For example, under McCain-Feingold it is a *felony* to run advertisements that even *mention* members of Congress 60 days prior to a federal election, much less criticize their actions. This applies to corporations, nonprofit issue advocacy groups such as the National Rifle Association and political "think tanks," labor unions, and pretty much everyone else. Moreover, the advertisements can't even include a photo or image of any member of Congress. It is *illegal* for a taxpayer advocacy group to run advertising that merely informs citizens how a sitting congressman voted with regard to tax increases. It is *illegal* for a pro-Second Amendment group to inform the public about the gun-control agenda of a sitting congressman. It is *illegal* for a pro-life group to advertise the pro-abortion statements of a sitting congressman. It is illegal for a group that champions traditional marriage to inform the public about legislation authored by a proponent of gay marriage in Congress.

In other words, thanks to McCain-Feingold, it is *illegal* for voters to make a truly informed decision on Election Day.

Obama and the Democrats crushed the McCain campaign in fundraising, allowing Obama to outspend McCain by a 3 to 1 margin across the board, and 7 to 1 in Indiana, 4 to 1 in Virginia, 2-1 in Ohio, and nearly 3 to 2 in North Carolina. Obama won all four of these critical battleground states.[3] Obama was able to raise unlimited funds because he turned down public financing for his campaign. McCain, on the other hand, opted to take federal tax dollars for his campaign.

Had conservative groups not been muzzled by McCain's own "reform" law, they just might have been able to help him close some of the gap in the months leading up to the election. Instead, Obama won in a landslide. Few Obama voters got to learn much about their candidate because:

1. McCain didn't have the money to counter Obama's ads, and

2. Conservative groups were barred from educating the public about the real Obama in the crucial two months prior to Election Day.

In addition, McCain's attack on free speech, a right that conservatives hold especially dear, forever alienated him from conservative support. Even if conservative groups had been legally permitted to run advertising in the run-up to the election, one wonders how forcefully they would have touted the credentials of the man who stripped them of their basic First Amendment freedom.

Because McCain-Feingold does not discriminate on the basis of political ideology—just on the basis of whether or not one is member of Congress—the bill has made strange bedfellows of liberal and conservative groups in court, as both ends of the political spectrum recognize the law's infringement on the First Amendment.

The ink bearing President Bush's signature on the bill was barely dry before it was challenged on constitutional grounds. Groups as diverse at the National Rifle Association and the American Civil Liberties Union banded together with individuals such as Sen. Mitch McConnell (R–KY) in *McConnell v. FEC* to challenge McCain-Feingold's constitutionality, and namely, its gross infringement on Americans' First Amendment rights

As NRA Executive Vice President Wayne LaPierre wrote after McCain-Feingold passed the Senate:

> NRA is not alone in being targeted for silence. The "issue advocacy" ban applies to every other lobbying organization in the nation—the ACLU, the Sierra Club, the Christian Coalition. Everybody is in the same boat. Unions as well...
>
> Everything in this awful legislation revolves around the "disbursement" and "expenditure" of money by groups like NRA or by unions or certain

for-profit corporations....

But John McCain's and the big media's attitude has been *damn the Constitution, full speed ahead*....

So the very concept in McCain's "reform" that an ad that "refers" to a candidate could be banned is, on its face, a violation of the right to free speech. (emphasis LaPierre)

In September 2003 the U.S. Supreme Court heard oral arguments in the case, and three months later, to the disappointment of free speech advocates, issued a 5-4 decision upholding the key provisions of McCain-Feingold. It is worth noting that this decision came before Justice Sandra Day O'Connor retired, and she sided with the court's anti-free speech wing to seal the First Amendment's fate.

Supreme Court Justice Antonin Scalia, one of the four dissenting justices in the case, authored a stinging opinion of the case's outcome. According to Scalia:

This is a sad day for the freedom of speech. Who could have imagined that the same Court which, within the past four years, has sternly disapproved of restrictions upon such inconsequential forms of expression as virtual child pornography, tobacco advertising, dissemination of illegally intercepted communications, and sexually explicit cable programming, would smile with favor upon a law that cuts to the heart of what the First Amendment is meant to protect: the right to criticize the government. For that is what the most offensive provisions of this legislation are all about. We are governed by Congress, and this legislation prohibits the criticism of Members of Congress by those entities most capable of giving such criticism loud voice: national political parties and corporations, both of the commercial and the not-for-profit sort...

This litigation is about preventing criticism of the government. I cannot say for certain that many, or some, or even any, of the Members of Congress who voted for this legislation did so not to produce "fairer" campaigns, but to mute criticism of their records and facilitate reelection...

The first instinct of power is the retention of power, and, under a Constitution that requires periodic elections, that is best achieved by the suppression of election-time speech.

According to an ATI-News/Zogby International poll that was conducted three months after the Supreme Court ruling, a strong majority of Americans sided with Justice Scalia. The poll asked: "The Supreme Court just ruled that corporations and organizations cannot buy advertising to air the record of a candidate for Congress or president within 60 days of the general election. However, the Supreme Court said that media organizations can promote candidates and issues on television and radio at any time they wish. Do you agree or disagree this gives a media-supported candidate an unfair advantage in a presidential or congressional contest?"

The verdict was clear as 70 percent of Americans agreed that McCain-Feingold creates an uneven playing field in federal elections and tilts favor toward media-backed candidates. Only 22 percent disagreed (the rest were "not sure"). Moreover, the majority was strong among Republicans (76 percent agreed), Democrats (63 percent agreed) and Independents (71 percent agreed).

Beginning of the End for McCain-Feingold?

In 2004, Wisconsin Right to Life (WRTL), a small grassroots group, ran several television advertisements that encouraged viewers to contact Sens. Russ Feingold and Herb Kohl, and ask them to cease filibustering Senate consideration of many of President Bush's judicial nominees. WRTL wanted to run the ads right up to the 2004 election, but was blocked from doing so by the FEC in its effort to implement the anti-free speech provision of McCain-Feingold.

In a 5-4 ruling, the U.S. Supreme Court sided with WRTL, making a distinction between "issue" ads (such as those WRTL wanted to run) and "advocacy" ads, which the court in 2002 narrowly ruled McCain-Feingold could prohibit. Justice Samuel Alito sat in place of anti-free speech Justice Sandra Day O'Connor, providing the crucial vote to tip the scales toward freedom.

Attorney Cleta Mitchell, who served as co-counsel to the National Rifle Association in *McConnell v. FEC*, was elated with the decision. In an article for *Human Events*, Mitchell wrote:

> For the first time in many years, a sliver of optimism has peeked out from behind the dark cloud of free speech suppression and political oppression brought to us courtesy of Sen. John McCain five years ago....
>
> The exciting thought struck longtime observers of this issue that maybe—just maybe—it might be that the Supreme Court was in the process of restoring the protections of the First Amendment to ordinary citizens and not just journalists, nude dancers and mushroom growers.
>
> The editorial and headline writers at the New York Times and Washington Post and their wannabes in other liberal newsrooms across the nation are in full swoon from their corporate perches, wringing their collective hands as they spew forth their concerns about the "corruption" caused by corporations—other than, of course, their own corporate media companies-by expressing political views... According to the New York Times and the "reform" cabal whose views are regularly parroted from the Times' corporate platform, the only corporation that should be allowed to speak freely on candidates, policies, issues, and legislation should be those in the news media business, such as, for instance, the New York Times....
>
> Sen. McCain issued a statement calling the Supreme Court's decision "regrettable," fearing, no doubt, that the ruling could well result in TV and

radio ads castigating him for his efforts on a myriad of issues that conservatives find wholly distasteful.

He isn't alone. Sen. Trent Lott (R.-Miss.) lamented recently the undue influence of conservative radio talk show hosts in opposing the Senate's proposed immigration legislation authored by (who else?) Sen. McCain. Sen. Dianne Feinstein (D.-Calif.) then opined that perhaps the "fairness doctrine" should be reinstated to mute the voices of conservative radio talk show hosts. There is a pattern here: Senators are seeking to silence citizens and critics, commentators and active opposition.[4]

Indeed, the WRTL ruling dealt a significant blow to politicians such as John McCain and Russell Feingold, who would rather rule high atop Capitol Hill without the inconvenience of being held accountable by the electorate. In a statement after the ruling, McCain lamented that now citizens and organizations would be free "to target a federal candidate in the days and weeks before an election."[5]

Of course, WRTL was merely attempting to exercise its First Amendment right to freedom of speech, and, as specifically safeguarded in the Amendment, to "petition the government for a redress of grievances." Such grievances have nothing to do with the phony "get corruption out of politics" battle cry of McCain, Feingold, and congressional Democrats who gave us the "Bipartisan Campaign Reform Act." Such grievances, however, have *everything* to do with holding politicians accountable for their actions.

McCain-Feingold Threatens to Shackle the World Wide Web

When the FEC drafted specific rules to implement McCain-Feingold in 2002, it voted 4-2 to exempt the Internet from its crackdown on political speech. Congress failed to list the Internet among the specific "public communications" that should be policed by the FEC, and thus, the majority of commissioners decided to spare the Web.[6]

Not to be content with anything but a thorough and complete crackdown on political speech, U.S. Reps. Christopher Shays (R-CT) and Martin Meehan (D-MA), who were the head cheerleaders of McCain-Feingold in the House, filed suit against the FEC in October 2002 to close a supposed Internet "loophole" in their bill. Not surprisingly, they were joined in their suit by Senators McCain and Feingold.[8]

In 2004, Federal Judge Colleen Kollar-Kotelly of the U.S. District Court for the District of Columbia agreed with Shays, Meehan, McCain, and Feingold, and sent the FEC back to the drawing board to devise how to ensnare Internet communications in its political speech dragnet. According to Judge Kollar-Kotelly, some Internet speech can be considered "public communication" under McCain-Feingold and should fall under the very broad catch-all stipulation in the bill that is meant to regulate and restrict "any other form of general public political advertising."[9]

The FEC board is evenly divided between the Republicans and Democrats, and the Republicans on the board were unsuccessful in convincing their Democratic counterparts to appeal Judge Kollar-Kotelly's ruling. Bradley A. Smith, then-commissioner of the FEC, recounts that the agency commenced a "bizarre" rulemaking process that, gone unreported and unchecked, could have been so sweeping as to clamp down on nearly all online communications—including blogs.[10] Ironically, however, a blog site sounded the alarm about the FEC's new rules, and sparked the outcry that prevented the rules from ever seeing the light of day.

According to media expert and author Adam Thierer:

> A first draft of the proposed FEC Web rules, leaked to the RedState blog in March 2006, would have regulated all but tiny, password-protected political sites, so bloggers had cause to be worried. Without a general exemption, political

blogs could easily find themselves in regulatory hell. Say it's a presidential race, Barack Obama versus John McCain. You run a wildly opinionated and popular group blog—call it No to Obama—that rails about the perils of an Obama presidency and sometimes republishes McCain campaign material. Is your blog making "contributions" to McCain? Maybe. The FEC, after all, says that a "contribution" includes "any gift, subscription, loan, advance, or deposit of money or *anything of value* made by any person for the purpose of influencing any election for Federal office."[11] (emphasis Thierer)

So, just as broadcasters lived in fear during the reign of the Fairness Doctrine, under these rules operators of websites, *including privately owned blogs*, could have had to cower under threats of FEC investigations, punishment and fines! As Thierer notes, "Most political bloggers aren't paid reporters or commentators; they're just ordinary citizens with day jobs who like to exercise their right to voice their opinions. If doing so without a lawyer puts them or their families at risk, many would simply stop blogging about politics—or never start."[12]

For example, during the 2008 campaign season, I constructed a website *(www.BarackObamaTest.com)* that allowed visitors to take a test to see if their views matched those of Obama on the critical issues of the day. The test questions were derived from questions that professional polling firms had asked Americans, and test takers could also see where the rest of America stood on the issues. In addition to being educational, the site was designed to promote my best-selling book, *The Audacity of Deceit: Barack Obama's War on American Values.*

The site was enormously popular, drawing roughly one million visitors over a span of merely six weeks. Of course, if the FCC had extended McCain-Feingold to the Internet, my site might never have existed. In fact, I was alerted later that the FEC had internal conversations about filing charges against me because of *BarackObamaTest.com.*

Such a scenario is hardly far-fetched, and it should sound familiar to those of us who remember the dark days of radio under the Fairness Doctrine.

Thankfully, once word spread about the FEC's plans for the Internet, both conservative and liberal bloggers and website operators cried foul and stopped the plans in their tracks. Instead of regulating online political speech, the FEC chose to mostly leave it alone. However, as Bradley Smith points out, "The biggest problem with the [new FEC] rules is simply the principle established—the internet is now to be subject to regulation."[13]

Smith is right. The camel's nose is permanently under the tent. The only hard and fast rule in campaign finance regulation is that the rules are ever-changing and subject to a federal judge's whim or that of a new administration. Now that President Obama is in office—given his track record of intolerance for any political speech that runs counter to his objectives—we can expect a renewed effort from the FEC to bring McCain-Feingold's command-and-control speech restrictions to the Internet.

Congressman Jeb Hensarling (R-TX) understands that the danger McCain-Feingold poses to free speech over the Internet, and in 2005, he introduced the Online Freedom of Speech Act. Sen. Harry Reid (D-NV) introduced the bill's companion in the Senate. The bill would have cemented the Internet's current unfettered status by immunizing blogs, other websites, and online communications from the campaign finance guillotine. Unfortunately, a strong majority of Democrats and a small band of liberal Republicans joined forces to kill the bill in November 2005.[14]

Ironically, supporters of McCain-Feingold are ignoring public opinion when it comes to so-called campaign finance reform. According to a 2008 Rasmussen Reports survey, only 22 percent think it would be a good idea to ban all campaign commercials so that voters could only get election campaign news from the news media and the Internet. On the other hand, 66 percent of Americans would rather have a potpourri of Election Year advertising than rely solely on the news media.[15]

Supreme Court Justice Clarence Thomas best summed up the devastating impact of McCain-Feingold with his stinging dissent in *McConnell v. FEC*:

> The First Amendment provides that "Congress shall make no law...abridging the freedom of speech." Nevertheless, the Court today upholds what can only be described as the most significant abridgment of the freedoms of speech and association since the Civil War. With breathtaking scope, the Bipartisan Campaign Reform Act of 2002 directly targets and constricts core political speech, the "primary object of First Amendment protection."...
>
> In response to this assault on the free exchange of ideas and with only the slightest consideration of the appropriate standard of review or of the Court's traditional role of protecting First Amendment freedoms, the Court has placed its imprimatur on these unprecedented restrictions....
>
> The chilling endpoint of the Court's reasoning is not difficult to foresee: outright regulation of the press. None of the rationales offered by the defendants, and none of the reasoning employed by the Court, exempts the press....
>
> Media companies can run pro-candidate editorials as easily as non-media corporations can pay for advertisements. Candidates can be just as grateful to media companies as they can be to corporations and unions. In terms of "the corrosive and distorting effects" of wealth accumulated by corporations that has "little or no correlation to the public's support for the corporation's political ideas," there is no distinction between a media corporation and a non-media corporation. Media corporations are influential. There is little doubt that the editorials and commentary they run can affect elections. Nor is there any doubt that media companies often wish to influence elections. One would think that the New York Times fervently hopes that its endorsement of Presidential candidates will actually influence people. What is to stop a future Congress from determining that the press is "too influential," and that the "appearance of corruption" is significant when media organizations endorse candidates or

run "slanted" or "biased" news stories in favor of candidates or parties? Or, even easier, what is to stop a future Congress from concluding that the availability of unregulated media corporations creates a loophole that allows for easy "circumvention" of the limitations of the current campaign finance laws?[16]

Now that the McCain-Feingold law looms over America's political landscape, the only barrier to further constitutional damage is a president and U.S. Congress dedicated to preserving our right to free speech. Unfortunately, at the moment we have neither.

Chapter Six
Sea of Voices

"The firmness with which the people have withstood the abuses of the press, the discernment they have manifested between truth and falsehood, show that they may safely be trusted to hear everything true and false, and to form a correct judgment between them."

—Thomas Jefferson, 1804

D URING HIS PRESIDENTIAL CAMPAIGN, Barack Obama displayed a stunning lack of tolerance for free speech.

One thing Americans can expect from an Obama administration, and a Democrat-controlled Congress, is a fight to re-establish censorship by bringing back the Fairness Doctrine. These politicians who fear free speech want to diminish alternative voices and ideas — namely those that are critical of liberal ideals and objectives — especially on talk radio.

According to an Obama spokesman during his 2008 campaign, the president believes any discussion of radio broadcasting should include "opening up the airwaves and modern communications to as many diverse viewpoints as possible…[and he] supports media-ownership caps, network neutrality, public broadcasting, as well as increasing minority ownership of broadcasting."[1] (That's gobbledygook for "restraint" and "censorship.")

What are Obama and his supporters capable of doing to his detractors, critics and opponents? Consider the case of Samuel Joseph Wurzelbacher, known during the 2008 presidential campaign as "Joe the Plumber." On a campaign swing through Wurzelbacher's neighborhood in Toledo, Ohio, Wurzelbacher asked Obama a question, on camera, about his plan to raise taxes on individuals and families making more than $200,000 a year — a plan that Wurzelbacher opposed. For his trouble, Obama surrogates, supporters, and print and television reporters sought to destroy Joe and publicly embarrass him by digging through his tax files, work history, divorce, and personal life. Was that a warning to average Americans not to ask questions?

Obama forces also tried to hush the National Rifle Association when it sought to run TV and radio ads exposing Obama's position on the issue of gun rights and the Second Amendment. In that instance, Obama's general counsel, Robert F. Bauer, fired off a letter September 23, 2008, threatening the licenses of broadcast stations that didn't pull the ad "for the sake of FCC licensing and the public interest."[2]

"This advertisement knowingly misleads your viewing audience about Senator Obama's position on the Second Amendment," the letter said. "We request that you immediately cease airing this advertisement."[3]

When Pittsburgh radio station KDKA host Kevin Miller gave air time to guests who were critical of Obama, his producer reprimanded him on the air and read a statement from CBS accusing Miller of unfair bias against Obama. The producer then offered Obama his own three-hour segment to run in place of Miller's time slot.

Following a dip in the polls in September, the Obama campaign dispatched prosecutors and law enforcement officials in Missouri to act as "truth squads," with a mission to target anyone who ran ads on television or radio critical of the Illinois Democrat.

In another campaign-related incident, when the tax-exempt 527 group the American Issues Project came out with a commercial linking Obama to former domestic terrorist William Ayers of the Vietnam War-era Weathermen Underground organization, Obama's campaign — unsuccessfully — "complained to the Department of Justice that AIP had broken campaign finance laws, and managed to spook some stations away from the ad," IBD reported.[4]

As a presidential candidate, Obama was bound by the rules already in place, and therefore, could do only so much to stifle any speech that he and his surrogates deemed detrimental to his campaign. The Obama camp was mostly relegated to filing complaints, threatening lawsuits, and organizing angry mobs to intimidate talk radio hosts.

As president, however, Obama is now in a powerful position to use the FCC to put talk radio, and any other speech he finds threatening to his re-election and his party's grip on power, out to pasture. There's no need to go through all the work of lawsuit filings and angry mob organizing when you can effectively muzzle the opposition by fiat.

This is why many politicians find stifling speech so tempting. They want to maintain their grip on power. Saying that, of course, would be a faux pas, so they have to make up other arguments for the need to stamp out free speech. Some, like Democratic Congressman Dennis Kucinich of Ohio, claim there are too few choices—so they want to squelch speech. To other politicians, there are *too many* choices—so they want to squelch speech. Their inconsistent reasoning aside, one thing is certain: The Left wants to squelch speech that is not lockstep with their values, their truths, their opinions.

Voices, voices everywhere

The truth is, "we live in a world of unprecedented media abundance—what once would have been the stuff of science fiction novels," writes Adam Thierer, in an editorial in the *Chicago Sun-Times*. "We can obtain and consume whatever media we want, wherever and whenever we want: television, radio, newspapers, magazines, and the bewildering variety of material available on the Internet."[5]

It's true. Those who argue there aren't enough voices can't seriously make a case for their argument. We already know there is an abundance of radio stations today—nearly double what existed in 1970. And let's not forget *satellite radio*; Jupiter Research predicts there will be 55 million subscribers to satellite radio by 2010.[6] And 86 percent of households subscribe to either cable or satellite television, receiving an average of 102 channels.[7] And, of course, there's the liberal, taxpayer-funded PBS.

In 2005, there were 18,267 magazines published, up from 14,302 in 1993.[8] In fact, writes Thierer, "the only declining media sector is the newspaper business."[9]

Where today's new voices are *really* sprouting up in remarkable numbers is the Internet. The Internet Systems Consortium notes that the number of Internet host computers — computers or servers that allow people to post content on the Web — has climbed to an astonishing 400 million-plus machines, Thierer says. And by mid-2007, Web data tracker Technorati said there were approximately 15.5 million active (liberal and conservative) blogs.[10]

A healthy marketplace

Indeed, by any measure, there certainly is no absence of disparate voices in the United States today. In fact, it's safe to say our country "has become as information-rich as any in society," says Thierer.[11]

And yet, despite an abundance of voices in the marketplace, too many lawmakers and regulators alike believe that the American state of media is abysmal. Some argue that media "localism" died a long time ago. Others say there is a lack of "diversity," and that too many groups and niches are going underserved.

Others, by comparison, actually say there are *too many* voices out there, and that because there are so many, it is impossible for a wide range of ideas to be heard. Still others say the market is "hopelessly over-concentrated in the hands of a few evil media barons who are hell-bent on forcefeeding us corporate propaganda."[12]

The fact is, nearly everyone has an opinion about "The Media." That's because there is some form of media presence — or, more often than not, *several* forms of media presence — in our everyday lives. And everyone has an opinion about the media — a fact that has probably endured throughout our nation's history.

"The first accusation of press bias surely flew the day the first newspaper was published," says press critic and *Slate* editor-at-large Jack Shafer.[13] Political scientist Mary Stuckey further argues, "Public discourse about the media tends toward the apocalyptic, and the media are convenient scapegoats for the myriad ills that are thought to assail us."[14]

Ultimately, media criticism often gives way to cries for regulation, especially from parties thought to be slighted or who don't believe their voice is being sufficiently heard.

"[M]edia regulation, in the form of structural ownership rules, market limitations, licensing or 'localism' requirements, speech restrictions or mandates, and so on — provides the means for critics to exert control over the media, or to reshape the media marketplace in their preferred image," says one analysis of today's media bazaar.[15] That concept would explain why there has been bipartisan support in Congress in the recent past for new media regulations. There has even been some bipartisan support for reinstating the Fairness Doctrine, though liberals in Congress by far outnumber conservatives in seeking its return.

Despite the varied reasons for wanting to curb free speech, critics who say there aren't enough voices to choose from are not dealing in reality. Once upon a time human beings were devoid of information, and what news and information they did receive was never timely. Oftentimes when news broke, it had already become dated and irrelevant. "Information spread at a snail's pace," according one analysis. "Few knew how to find printed materials, assuming that they even knew how to read."[16]

None of that is true today. Consider this analysis from telecommunications expert and author Clay Shirky:

> We are living in the middle of the largest increase in expressive capability in the history of the human race. More people can communicate more things to more people than has ever been possible in the past, and the size and speed of this increase, from under one million participants to over one billion in a generation, makes the change unprecedented, even considered against the background of previous revolutions in communications tools.[17]

By any reasonable measure, media diversity is getting *better* for Americans, not *worse*.

"To the extent that there was ever a 'golden age' of media in America, we are living it today," one extensive analysis of today's media climate concluded.[18] There is more media choice, more competition, more variety than ever.

Range of delivery, range of storage

Further supporting the argument that there is a plethora of media today, not a dearth, you must examine the distribution of media, the way it is received, and the way it is stored for later use and consumption. In 1970, for instance, choices were much more limited, though that's not to say there were few choices.

Consumers mostly received news and information via what we'd consider "traditional" sources today—broadcast television and radio, print newspapers and magazines. Media marketing also encompassed theaters and cinemas, records and tapes, and books.

Fast-forward a few decades to the present time. Not only are those "traditional" forms of media delivery still in use—though some, like print publications, are fading—there are many more choices on television (to now include cable and satellite), as well as many more voices on radio (AM/FM/cable/satellite). There is also the Internet and its numerous websites and personal blogs, wireless networks to serve both personal computers, and cell phones that become more sophisticated by the year. Satellite and cable operators are delivering multiple media layers to homes to include television, the Internet, and telephone service. Portable, digital cameras can capture and record moments in history for instant broadcast worldwide via the Internet. Chat rooms and instant messaging both add to the immediacy of delivering content and ideas, and serve as debate platforms. Records have gone the way of the Dodo bird, but they have been replaced by CDs and digital delivery platforms; new songs, for example, can be released in mere moments to a global audience—and from just about anywhere in the world—via wireless Internet delivery. websites like ATI-News.com can bring Internet users news from all over the world.

Indeed, there are more devices available to broadcast media every year.

"Some critics like to wax nostalgic about a supposed golden age of media when the citizenry was supposedly far better informed and more engaged in deliberative democracy," says an analysis by Adam Thierer and co-analyst Grant Eskelsen, in their special report, "Media Metrics: The True State of the Modern Media Marketplace." "But that's wishful thinking at best and revisionist history at worst. The fact is, we are far better informed today than were our ancestors."[19]

And though the veracity of the content can often be questionable, "a weekday edition of The New York Times contains more information than the average person was likely to come across in a lifetime in seventeenth-century England," writes Richard Saul Wurzman, author of *Information Anxiety*.[20]

Too *many* voices?

But there are those who believe too *much* media is *not* a good thing. Their argument is baffling; they believe too many voices mean too *few* choices. And, they argue, too few media corporations own too many outlets, thereby endangering choice.

In 2002, Todd Gitlin, a professor at Columbia University in New York and an author who argues that there is too much media, said this in response to a question from *Salon.com* about whether there was "an oversaturation point with the news, so that we no longer care about the real issues at hand":

> Definitely. Most Americans still think violent crime is increasing, when it isn't. The local news and the cop shows cultivate this fancy. Some of these binges have more staying power than others, but they suck all of the oxygen out of the mental room. So they contribute to a national attention deficit disorder.[21]

That seems a rather simplistic explanation for a much more complex issue. Gitlin is obviously a smart guy and he appears reasoned in his response. But he also seems to equate the consumption of reality shows, for example, with the pursuit of legitimate news and information—as if both genres of media were the same in content and source. Without sounding too obvious, it seems more appropriate to recognize that consumers of reality shows seek them out when that is the type of media they desire. It is also correct to note that reality show consumers could also be consumers of news and information, if in fact they are seeking news and information. The point is, consumers know the difference, and they should be free to make their own choices—while being given a range of choices to make. The free media market has provided a never-ending buffet for consumers.

Recent books by Gitlin and Barry Schwartz—*Media Unlimited: How the Torrent of Images and Sounds Overwhelms Our Lives,* and, *The Paradox of Choice: Why More Is Less*, respectively—"capture the anxiety felt by these opponents of media multiplicity," writes Thierer.[22]

As to the argument that too many media outlets are owned by too few interests, a 2002 FCC survey of 10 media markets—from the largest (New York City) to the smallest (Altoona, Pennsylvania)—showed that each had more outlets and owners in 2000 than in 1960. "And the FCC counted all of a market's cable channels as a single outlet (even though the typical viewer would regard each channel as a distinct one) and didn't include national newspapers or Internet sites as media sources, so the diversity picture was even brighter than it seemed," Thierer writes in an April 2007 article published in *City Journal*.[23]

No matter the argument—too much media, too little choice, too few owners—those who take any of those positions are all united in one solution: Foist new regulations on speech. It's just as simple as that. They seek to replace the sea of voices that became available once the Fairness Doctrine was mercifully lifted with a much more narrow, *defined* set of voices that *they* control, and that echo their own ideological beliefs.

That's not freedom. It's tyranny.

Chapter Seven
Failure of Left-wing Talk

"I learned a long time ago that when people or institutions begin to behave in a matter that seems to be entirely against their own interests, it's because we don't understand what their motives really are. It would seem that by so exposing their biases and betting everything on one candidate over another, the traditional media is trying to commit suicide—especially when, given our current volatile world and economy, the chances of a successful Obama presidency, indeed any presidency, is probably less than 50/50."

—Journalist Michael Malone, Oct. 24, 2008

A NGERED BY THE DOMINANCE of conservative talk radio and, most likely, exasperated by repeated failed attempts to bring back an outdated, unconstitutional policy that would force ideological competitors off the air, left-wing ideologues recently attempted a free-market solution to their problem of securing "equal time."

In the spring of 2004, an investment group bankrolled an experiment in like-minded talk radio, naming the new network "Air America," and set about trying to secure a place in the nation's largest radio markets alongside established conservative giants like Bill Bennett, Neal Boortz, Mark Levin, James Dobson, and Dennis Prager.

In 2002 Chicago-based, self-described "socially responsible venture capitalists" Sheldon and Anita Drobny, upset over the firing of a favorite radio host, Mike Malloy, decided to try to get him syndicated across the country. At Malloy's suggestion, the Drobnys initially contacted Atlanta-based radio executive, Jon Sinton, and made the pitch to get Malloy syndicated nationally. From there, the Drobnys hired Sinton to be the CEO of their newly formed company, AnShell Media, and the trio next concentrated on raising money for the new venture.

The first fundraiser was held in October 2002 at the home of the quite liberal Arianna Huffington, founder of the leftist online blog *The Huffington Post*—an event which drew a number of notables with deep pockets from the Hollywood scene. Sinton's brother, broadcaster Carey Bruce Sinton, suggested calling the new venture Central Air, a name that stuck until just before the network was formally launched.

The proposed network quickly found friends in the mainstream media and, as such, was treated to millions of dollars' worth of free advertising and marketing. The lavish adulation and praise began in earnest when AnShell publicly announced its intentions to form the new left-wing network in a *New York Times* article in February 2003. The paper's reporter, Jim Rutenberg, interviewed Jon Sinton about the supposed need for a balanced national dialogue on the airwaves.

"The object of the programming is to be progressive and make a statement that counters this din from the right," Sinton told the paper. "But we have a solid business plan that shows a hole in the market."[1] His plan was not to go after talk radio's gold standard, Rush Limbaugh, head-on. "You're not going to beat him at his game," he said. Rather, the plan was to feature programming with morning, afternoon, and early evening shows featuring hosts with as many big names in entertainment as possible.[2]

Initially raising $10 million in cash—enough, radio analysts told the small media group, to at least begin operations—the Drobnys incorporated fellow venture capitalist and Harvard Business School grad Javier Saade, and kept trying to raise money the rest of 2003.

At the same time, the group met frequently with *Saturday Night Live* alumnus and comedian Al Franken, eventually convincing him to become the new network's franchise talent.

Sinton also managed to land actress and liberal activist Janeane

Garofalo after mentioning her during an appearance on the CNN program *Politics Today*. Later, at a fundraising event in Los Angeles, Sinton—at Franken's suggestion—met with *Daily Show* co-creator Lizz Winstead and convinced her to join the newly forming managerial team as vice president of entertainment programming. About that same time, Sinton successfully recruited Shelley Lewis away from her job producing *American Morning* for CNN to serve with AnShell as vice president of new programming. By the fall of 2003, Sinton's brother Steve left Clear Channel's talk radio division to join the new company as vice president of programming and operations.

Fundraising, however, proved to be more difficult than initially imagined. During a trip to Washington, D.C., former chief of staff to President Bill Clinton and the chief of President Obama's transition team, John Podesta, suggested meeting with a lawyer, David Goodfriend, who then introduced the would-be progressive media moguls to his former college roommate, Evan Montvel Cohen. Cohen had done well handling advertising and research companies in the Pacific Rim. At that point, having gone as far as they could with the new concept, AnShell's principles sold their interests to Cohen and his partner, Rex Sorensen, a Guam-based broadcaster, who together formed Progress Media, with Cohen acting as its chairman and Mark Walsh its CEO. Sinton remained on as president.

Early in 2004, talent, engineers and producers were hired and a lease was signed with New York's 1190 WLIB-AM, creating a home in the nation's largest market and the company's first affiliate. Air America Radio (AAR) was officially launched at noon Eastern time on March 31, 2004.

Talent, management problems

Sinton was quickly able to assemble a national network of 100 radio stations, including 18 of the top 20 markets, in just six months — making AAR the fastest growing network in modern radio history.

But AAR soon began having problems, not the least of which were related to funding.

When it launched, AAR officials claimed the network had secured $30 million in venture capital; that amount was later estimated by *The Wall Street Journal* to be closer to $6 million, with Sorensen claiming an important investor had backed out at the last minute.

Two weeks after launch, AAR programming was discontinued in a pair of key markets over contract disputes. Nearly one month to the day later, AAR ended broadcasting on WNTD-AM in Chicago over contract problems. And the network lost a court battle with Multicultural Radio, which owned two stations that initially contracted to carry AAR programming, which really cost the fledgling left-wing network.

Four weeks after launch, AAR's CEO, Mark Walsh, and its executive vice president for programming, Dave Logan, left the network. A week later, its chairman Evan Cohen and vice chairman and investment partner Rex Sorenson, were forced out by the remaining investors, who then asked Sinton and AAR's executive producer, Carl Ginsburg, a lawyer and experienced newsman, to operate the network.

Things only got worse. Leadership, as well as ownership, was changed again. By February 2005, a new CEO, Danny Goldberg, was named, and in April that same year, Gary Krantz was named the network's new president. Ginsburg and Sinton were named co-chief operations officers; Ginsburg was put in charge of operations and Sinton in charge of programming and affiliate relations.

Continued problems between on-air talent and management led to further unrest, and by April 2006, Goldberg announced he was leaving the company after a little more than a year on the job.

Besides management, talent was also changing—and bailing out.

Garofalo's last day on the air as co-host of *The Majority Report* came in July 2006; rumors flew that she, too, was having strained relations with management. Mike Malloy and Randi Rhodes soon left as well. Malloy landed on a new liberal talk network called Nova M Radio in 2006 and Rhodes joined him in 2008.

Money woes

Despite denials that were quite vehement at times, Air America Radio eventually did file for Chapter 11 bankruptcy protection on October 13, 2006. According to court filings, the company at the time had about $4.3 million in assets but more than $20 million in liabilities. Host Franken alone was owed more than $360,000 in salary; Rob Glaser, founder of RealNetworks (an Internet streamer known for such products as RealAudio and RealPlayer) was owed a staggering $9.8 million. The filing had over 25 pages of creditors and showed that the company lost $9.1 million in 2004, $19.6 million in 2005 and an additional $13.1 million by mid-October in 2006.[3]

Financially speaking, there was also a hint of corruption. In July 2005, the *Bronx News* reported that the Gloria Wise Boys and Girls Clubs of Co-op City, a nonprofit group that provided services for children and seniors in the Bronx, New York, loaned $480,000 to then-owner of AAR, Progress Media. Later it was discovered that there had been four separate money transfers from Gloria Wise: $80,000; $87,000; $218,000; and $490,000—all between October 2, 2003, and March 14, 2004, totaling $875,000. Moreover, no interest had been paid on these loans. Host Franken, along with one-time chairman Evan Cohen, were among the signers of the confidential agreement.[4]

The loans became part of an investigation by New York state officials.

"Transfers to Air America from Gloria Wise, for which Mr. Cohen worked as a fund-raiser during the period when he helped launch the liberal network, have surfaced as part of the probe by the city's Department of Investigation and the state attorney general into 'inappropriate transactions' by Gloria Wise," *The New York Sun* reported. "The city has frozen all grants and contracts with the organization, which had an annual budget of $20 million, and many of its programs have been reassigned to other Bronx organizations."[5]

AAR was also sold a number of times, almost always because the current owners needed new funding in order to keep operations afloat. But money problems always came down to one thing: not enough listeners cared for the network's shrill, left-wing drivel. Ratings were in the tank, and revenues from advertising were barely a trickle.

Even though conservatives were being battered relentlessly by the mainstream media during the waning years of the Bush administration; even though the Bush White House was suffering through some of the poorest approval ratings in presidential history (much of that, no doubt, driven by the relentless battering of the mainstream media); and even though Democrats were winning control of both Houses of Congress (in 2006) and the White House (in 2008); left-wing radio *still* couldn't make any headway with the American people.

Why?

"If conventional wisdom were correct, one would believe that America is shifting to the left out of disgust over the job being done by President Bush and Republicans in Congress," wrote pundit Bill Niehuis, in an April 2006 blog post. "That should mean that fewer people would be attracted to conservative talk radio and other media, right? That should mean that networks like Air America should be beating the pants off personalities like Rush Limbaugh and Sean Hannity, right? Wrong. Where are the liberals?"[6]

According to data obtained and published by Matt Drudge on his Drudge Report website, liberals *aren't* in the marketplace of ideas:

> Left-leaning new media has hit turbulence at the marketplace, newly released stats show. A book hyped by major media as documenting a progressive revolution of "blogs" and political power, DAILY KOS 'CRASHING THE GATE' has sold only 3,630 copies since its release (in March 2006), according to NIELSEN's BOOKSCAN. [NIELSEN claims only 2,062 copies of DAILY KOS have been purchased at the retail level; the rest coming through 'discount' outlets.] Meanwhile, the just-released radio Winter Book [Jan-March 2006] from ARBITRON shows AIR AMERICA in New York City losing more than a third of its audience — in the past year! Among all listeners 12+, it was a race to the bottom for AIR AMERICA and WLIB as middays went from a 1.6 share during winter 2005 to a 1.0 share winter 2006.[7]

By winter 2008, ratings for the entire network weren't much better. Air America stations carrying a majority AAR programming and in markets for which Arbitron reports results four times a year averaged a 1.2 share.

By comparison, in the spring of 2008 *Talkers Magazine* listed Rush Limbaugh, Sean Hannity, Michael Savage, Dr. Laura Schlessinger, Glenn Beck, Laura Ingraham and Mark Levin in the top spots respectively. At the bottom were known liberals like Alan Colmes, Randi Rhodes, Thom Hartmann, and Lionel (born Hiawatha Lipschitz) — most of them AAR or former AAR "talent."[8]

Liberals, both on the air and off, have blamed everyone from Rush Limbaugh to the Republican Party for their failure to make inroads on the airwaves. Such consistently dismal showings, along with AAR's reliably poor ratings and performance, once again explain why the radical leftists want to force their way into the marketplace by re-implementing the

Fairness Doctrine. It's because they know they can't compete on a level playing field. Clearly, Americans have made their preference known.

The reality is it's no secret why tens of millions of Americans have flocked to conservative talk radio. It is one of the few media formats where they can hear alternative ideas. They can't get them in the major newspapers. They can't find them in most mass market magazines. They can't get them on network newscasts. They can't get them in entertainment media. The 2008 presidential election, and the mainstream media's obvious love affair with Barack Obama, proved that beyond a doubt.

The reason talk radio listenership flourished rather than declined during the 2008 elections is that Americans could not find any positive news about the president or Republicans anywhere else. In the face of what was repeatedly sold by the mainstream media as a failed Bush presidency and Republican leadership, they knew instinctively that they wouldn't get the straight scoop from the *New York Times, Washington Post, Los Angeles Times, Time,* or *Newsweek.*

The constant drumbeat of negativity was encapsulated perfectly by left-wing journalist Joe Klein, in his November 26, 2008 *Time* magazine article:

> We have "only one President at a time," Barack Obama said in his debut press conference as President-elect. Normally, that would be a safe assumption — but we're learning not to assume anything as the charcoal-dreary economic winter approaches. By mid-November, with the financial crisis growing worse by the day, it had become obvious that one President was no longer enough (at least not the President we had). ... And yet this final humiliation seems particularly appropriate for George W. Bush. At the end of a presidency of stupefying ineptitude, he has become the lamest of all possible ducks.[9]

With consistently negative coverage like that, it's no surprise that tens of millions of Americans who simply did not agree with such views, or who viewed such comments as ridiculously skewed, would ultimately seek out a medium that at least presented another side of the issues. And AAR, as well as other "progressive" radio formats, was never that alternative. In fact, all Air America Radio represents is a continuation of the biased coverage offered in mainstream media.

Liberal bias in the mainstream is what gave rise to talk radio in the first place, notes *LA Times* columnist Brian Anderson. "People turn to it to help right the imbalance," he says.[10]

Moreover, say others, AAR — like all other liberal talk on the radio waves — was doomed to fail.

"Air America's problem is that it is an artificially generated public-relations ploy. Prior to its inception, the open market clearly did not demand a high-profile, left-wing radio network, or else one would have evolved on its own," said Guy Benson, the conservative co-host of Chicago station WNUR-FM's *Feedback* program, at the time of AAR's launch. "The fact that a small group of wealthy liberal elites decided that such a network was necessary means very little."[11]

Finally, AAR — and liberal talk in general — fail because of their tone, tenor and content. How many times a day can you hear a host whine, "George Bush is a dummy," and "Iraq was a mistake," before you get bored and move onto something else? The Left has made a career out of hating President Bush; when the conversation turned to solutions, however, left-wingers didn't have much to offer.

But now that they have returned to power they will have to lay out their strategies.

And will AAR be their voice on the radio waves?

Not for much longer, if the network's short history is any guide. Unless, of course, the network gets a legislative leg-up from the ruling party in Congress and the White House.

Chapter Eight

Conservative Success on the Air

"As the founding president of Air America Radio, I believe that for the last eight years Rush Limbaugh and his ilk have been cheerleaders for everything wrong with our economic, foreign and domestic policies. But when it comes to the Fairness Doctrine, I couldn't agree with them more. The Fairness Doctrine is an anachronistic policy that, with the abundance of choices on radio today, is entirely unnecessary."

—Jon Sinton, Founding President of *Air America Radio*[1]

IN THE DECADES when the Fairness Doctrine was the law of the land, right-thinkers were largely banished from the bastions of the establishment media. No matter how hard they tried to be heard, their ideas were drowned out by a combination of liberal newspeak, politically correct thinking, and command messages from the headquarters of the Left: the *New York Times*, the *Washington Post*, and the big three network newscasts.

Perhaps the conservative who learned those tough lessons the fastest was Rush Limbaugh. "In 1987," says an editorial by Daniel Henninger in the *Wall Street Journal*, Limbaugh "sat down at a microphone at radio station KFBK-AM in Sacramento and began broadcasting something called 'The Rush Limbaugh Show.' The rest is history."[2]

Indeed it is, and it's a history that is still being written today, more than 21 years later. Limbaugh was the first political talk-format broadcaster to take advantage of President Reagan's decision to kill the Fairness Doctrine. Unencumbered by the old rules mandating "equal time" for ideological rivals—while the mainstream media continued to play its role—the talk pioneer smashed through the din of the Left, attracting millions of listeners who, for the first time, were able to finally hear the other side of the story.

"In a real sense, one can say that he created the art form and has been its star performer" ever since, writes William G. Mayer, in a 2004 *Public Interest* piece examining conservative talk radio.[3]

Many others have followed in his footsteps, and today their programs and like-minded ideology dominate talk radio, to the chagrin of the Left. How this phenomenon occurred is both a model of success—delivering a product no one else was delivering but for which there clearly was, and continues to be, a need—and a testament to liberty.

Model for success

Before their domination of talk radio, were conservatives tilting at left-wing windmills? Was all the liberal bias in the media and academia simply imagined? To dismiss conservative criticism of the mainstream media is to ignore the immense success and popularity of conservative ideology on the radio and, increasingly, online.

"In 1994, Newt Gingrich, his Contract With America and the Republicans regained control of the House of Representatives for the first time since 1952—the years in which the Fairness Doctrine largely kept politics off the air," writes Henninger. "This didn't happen because the Gingrich candidates were getting their message out in the *Los Angeles Times* or *Boston Globe*."[4]

Media expert Brian C. Anderson, in his book, *South Park Conservatives: The Revolt Against Liberal Media Bias*, "cites left-wing philosopher Herbert Marcuse (who taught at Columbia, Harvard and Brandeis) urging liberals [during the 1960s] to practice active 'intolerance against movements from the Right' in the name of 'liberating tolerance.' Thus, for example, liberal academics would vote to deny tenure for conservative colleagues—and still do—believing that this is a *morally mandated* act."[5]

The mainstream media, and those on the political Left who criticize the conservative dominance of talk radio while pining for "progressive" alternatives to Rush Limbaugh, Glenn Beck, G. Gordon Liddy, Janet Parshall, Phil Valentine, Kirby Wilbur and Hugh Hewitt, et al, really have no one to blame but themselves for the dramatic success of conservative talk. They are responsible for its creation.

In a detailed special report titled, "Unmasking the Myths Behind the Fairness Doctrine," the Media Research Center provides insight into why conservative talk radio does so well. Quite simply, it is because there is virtually no media venue for conservative ideology on television.

"Major liberal-leaning sources of news and opinion reach a far greater audience than conservative-leaning sources," the report says.[6] Consider the following listenership, readership and viewership figures:[7]

- Broadcast TV news, millions/day: Liberal 42.1, Conservative 0

- Top 25 newspapers, millions/day: Liberal 11.7, Conservative 1.3

- Cable TV news, millions/month: Liberal 182.8, Conservative 61.6

- Top talk radio, millions/week: Liberal 24.5, Conservative 87.0

- Newsweeklies, millions/week: Liberal 8.5, Conservative 0

So, you see, virtually the only traditional media venue where conservative ideology gets a fair shake is talk radio.

But the reason that conservatism has succeeded so wildly on the airwaves is not entirely due to ideology, say experts. There are a number of reasons why.[8]

Entertainment value. Let's face it, the mavericks of conservative talk are *just more entertaining.* Even some of Rush Limbaugh's most vehement critics acknowledge that he is a consummate professional broadcaster who brings enormous talent to his daily three-hour program. "At least part of Limbaugh's audience, according to several surveys, consists of people who disagree with what he says but simply find him entertaining," writes Mayer.[9]

Says Anderson, "The top conservative hosts put on snazzy, frequently humorous shows. Kathleen Hall Jamieson, dean of the University of Pennsylvania's Annenberg School for Communication, observes: 'The parody, the asides, the self-effacing humor, the bluster are all part of the packaging that makes the political message palatable.' Besides, the triumph of political correctness on the left makes it hard for on-air liberals to lighten things up without offending anyone."[10]

Dr. Rob Balon, chief executive officer of Benchmark Company, which conducted an independent national study of 997 AM and FM radio listeners in the top 100 markets in 2003, said of the study's results regarding talk radio, "While the number of nationally syndicated shows has grown in the past decade, the driving factor for listeners is talent, not ideology. Rush Limbaugh works because he is a talented entertainer who puts a great deal of effort into preparation so that he hosts a good show. He just happens to be a conservative."[11]

Some would argue Balon's comments regarding the appeal, or non-appeal, of Limbaugh's ideology as a reason for his success, but again, this simple truth about liberal talk radio remains relevant: How "entertaining" is it to listen to a host do nothing but snipe for hours on end?

Dividing target audiences. The potential audience for liberals is much smaller than for conservatives, because of the mediums already serving them ideologically.[12] "Large percentages of liberals are black and Hispanic, and they now have their own specialized entertainment radio outlets, which they aren't likely to leave for liberal talk radio," explains political consultant Dick Morris.[13] Anderson adds, "The potential audience for

Air America or similar ventures is thus pretty small—white liberals, basically. And they've already got NPR."

Old media liberal bias. Because of it, people have turned to talk radio to right what they perceive as an ideological imbalance in the media overall.[15]

However influential Limbaugh may be, "the conservative dominance of the medium…extends well beyond" their programs, Mayer observed:

> Sean Hannity, for example, has an audience only slightly smaller than Limbaugh's, yet whatever Hannity's other talents, no one has ever called him a 'master showman.' And is creative talent really so scarce among liberals that after at least a decade of searching, they have been unable to find a single left-leaning talk show host with enough pizzazz to establish a modest national following?[16]

Some say conservative talk has been so successful because talk radio is a medium which cultivates clear, concise, straightforward discussion of the issues—a task at which conservatives in particular are very skilled. Liberal positions, some argue, are much more complex and nuanced and, thus, harder to explain in the kind of black-and-white terms prevalent on conservative programs.[17] Victor Navasky, the longtime editor of the left-wing magazine *The Nation,* said, "Radio is a sound bite medium, and the Left does not have a sound bite program."[18] Former Democratic U.S. Sen. Gary Hart of Colorado, himself a short-lived talk show host, agreed: "Progressive politics in this country has failed to compress the message, and I'm not sure that it can. Because by definition, the reformer, the progressive, the liberal, whatever you want to call it, doesn't see the world in blacks and whites, but in plaids and grays. There never is a single simple answer. It is always a set of interrelated policies."[19]

That argument, of course, is as incorrect as it is pompous and arrogant—both traits of which characterize politicians and liberal talk radio. Any reasonable person, say talk radio analysts, would have to disavow such a preposterous theory when you consider that some of the genre's most successful talkers include the following:

• Laura Ingraham, a Dartmouth College and University of Virginia law school grad, lawyer and former Reagan administration speechwriter who served as a law clerk to Supreme Court Justice Clarence Thomas and Ralph K. Winter on the U.S. Court of Appeals for the Second Circuit; and

• William Bennett, a former education secretary in the Reagan administration, and the nation's first "drug czar" in President George H. W. Bush's Office of National Drug Control Policy—to name just a few of his scores of governmental and academic accomplishments.[20]

Others argue that conservatives dominate the airwaves because the only true liberal voices of any significance come from a generally overlooked source: so-called "shock jocks" who largely reside on the FM side of the dial, like Howard Stern and "Mancow" Mullen.

"Shock jocks are this country's progressive talkers, ranting for hours on end on behalf of civil liberties, sexual freedom, the rights of the little guy against the nation's big corporations and institutions (and—sorry, Dems—against affirmative action)," Marc Fisher argued in a February 2003 article on *Slate.com*.[21]

That explanation is as simplistic as it is incorrect. To hold up Stern and Mancow as prototypical "progressives" is ludicrous. While it can be said truthfully that Stern, for instance, is no crusader for traditional morality, his political views certainly can't be pigeonholed as liberal/ progressive. Howard Kurtz, who covers the media for the *Washington Post,* provided a summary on Stern's political views:

He talked about how Social Security was a "big scam," being ripped off by retirees who were secretly working, and how his generation was "never gonna see it anyway." He denounced George Bush for being anti-abortion, saying any woman who voted for him might as well mail her vagina to the White House. He chatted with Jennifer Flowers. He said the L.A. police were right to beat Rodney King. He played the taped messages of a Ku Klux Klan organizer, ridiculing him at every turn. He pronounced O.J. Simpson guilty and wondered if a black jury would let him off the hook. He was anti-government, anti-drugs, anti-welfare, anti-immigrant. He made fun of blacks, Jews, homosexuals, and the handicapped.[22]

In the weeks leading up to the 2004 presidential election, Stern did begin heaping more abuse on President Bush while saying a few positive things about Democratic Sen. John Kerry of Massachusetts, his opponent. But even that small praise didn't represent a sea change in political views for Stern. "His real gripe against the [Bush] administration stems not from its policies about taxes or terrorism, but from the attempt by the Federal Communications Commission to fine his program for indecent content (Editor's note: Clear Channel, one of Stern's syndicators, was fined $495,000 in April 2004; in response, the company booted him off its six stations carrying his program. Sirius Satellite Radio offered him a 5-year, $500 million deal; he began his show with Sirius in January 2006)."[23]

As for Mancow, who is based in Chicago, he had been writing occasional columns that were archived at the conservative news website *Newsmax.com*—columns that were critical of former President Bill Clinton and uber-leftist Hollywood fixture Barbara Streisand.[24]

Plus, for liberals to insist there isn't any like-minded talk on radio waves is simply inaccurate. By any responsible measure, most talk programming on the taxpayer-funded National Public Radio (NPR) network is very left-wing, and NPR is broadcast in most major markets to a weekly audience of 26 million listeners.

Still others say liberals don't do well on the air because the big corporate networks who own the stations are all conservatives.

"There are a lot of phony excuses for why the right wing dominates [talk radio], but the most obvious, true explanation is that the management at these stations is conservative," Jeff Cohen, executive director of the left-wing media watchdog group Fairness and Accuracy in Reporting, told the *New York Times*.[25]

But the bottom line concerning the success of conservative talk radio is *the bottom line*. In truth, media owners will broadcast just about anything that attracts listeners and increases their subscription numbers or advertising revenue. Ideological content has less to do with it than you might imagine. Consider one example in CBS's broadcast of *60 Minutes*, a program that "takes a relentlessly critical view of corporate and business behavior," according to one analysis.[26] The reason is that *60 Minutes* gets consistently good ratings and has, over the years, retained a sizeable audience, media analyst Mayer noted.[27]

The same principle applies to talk radio shows. Corporations and radio stations broadcast conservative talk shows because they attract huge audiences and make money; liberal shows do neither, generally speaking.

Boston Globe columnist Alex Beam provided an example of this theory in practice:

> Colin McEnroe lost his talk show gig with WTIC in Hartford (Connecticut) a few years ago, dumped in favor of Laura Schlessinger (he has since been rehired). McEnroe is vaguely liberal and assumed he was being ditched as part of the rightward drift in radio. "It turned out my bosses' politics weren't that different from mine," McEnroe says. "All they cared about was the ratings.
>
> If Noam Chomsky playing the kazoo on air got them 11 ratings, they would put him on."[28]

Content, entertainment value, and market share—all strong reasons why conservative talk consistently does well and why liberal talk fails.

It's also why enemies of free expression and speech are so intolerant of talk radio—because it represents the greatest challenge to their ideology. They have decided if they can't compete with conservatives in the talk radio medium, they prefer to force them into compliance.

Or, more accurately, into silence.

Chapter Nine
Beyond Talk Radio

"A system of limitless individual choices, with respect to communications, is not necessarily in the interest of citizenship and self-government."

—President Obama's Regulatory Czar, Cass Sunstein, arguing that a Fairness Doctrine is needed for the Internet, in his book, *Republic.com 2.0*

U P TO NOW, most of the debate over a return of the Fairness Doctrine has focused on what its impact would be regarding talk radio. And, based on historical data and the evidence since the doctrine's demise, should lawmakers reimpose the doctrine its affect on the talk radio medium would be immediate and disastrous.

There is no question that a return of the doctrine would once again rein in free expression and the unimpeded exchange of competing ideas because, as before, radio station managers, program directors, and networks would simply return to broadcasting "vanilla" programming that contained nothing controversial, nothing interesting, and nothing political. In fact, some industry analysts think a sizable portion of radio stations, especially those on the AM side of the dial, would go the way of the Dodo bird. Before Rush Limbaugh salvaged the medium, AM broadcasting was already headed for extinction.

But what is even more chilling is that many believe the Fairness Doctrine would be expanded to include other communications mediums that some politicians have found particularly problematic.

"There's a huge concern among conservative talk radio hosts that reinstatement of the Fairness Doctrine would all but destroy the industry due to equal time constraints," writes Jeff Poor of the

Business & Media Institute. "But speech limits might not stop at radio. They could even be extended to include the Internet and 'government dictating content policy.'"[1]

Poor says that distinct possibility was raised when FCC Commissioner Robert McDowell spoke to bloggers at the Heritage Foundation in Washington, D.C. in August 2008. He says McDowell spoke about "a recent FCC vote to bar Comcast from engaging in certain Internet practices—expanding the federal agency's oversight of Internet networks."[2] McDowell, a Bush appointee, said he was against the Comcast reprimand, and said the "Net neutrality requirement could ultimately win over a few conservatives who may not fully understand the implications of the rule—and the long-term effects of government regulation."

McDowell noted:

> I think the fear is that somehow large corporations will censor their content, their point of view, right. I think the bigger concern for them should be if you have government dictating content policy, which by the way would have a big First Amendment problem. Then, whoever is in charge of government is going to determine what is fair, under a so-called 'Fairness Doctrine,' which won't be called that—it'll be called something else. So, will websites, will bloggers have to give equal time or equal space on their website to opposing views, rather than letting the marketplace of ideas determine that?[3]

At the time, McDowell said re-implementing the Fairness Doctrine wasn't on the radar screen of the FCC. But he cautioned that a new administration and congressional majority, such as those which were swept into power in November 2008, could push for a new doctrine of equal or expanded reach.

"So you know," McDowell warned, "this election, if it goes one way, we could see reimposition of the Fairness Doctrine. There is a discussion of it in Congress. I think it won't be called the Fairness Doctrine by folks who are promoting it. I think it will be called something else and I think it'll be intertwined into the net neutrality debate."[4]

In fact, there has already been an effort to control content online, under the excuse of wanting to control "indecency." And it was a bipartisan effort.

In February 1995 Sens. Jim Exon (D-NE) and Slade Gorton (R-WA) introduced the Communications Decency Act. The measure called for fines of up to $250,000 and two years imprisonment for anyone who, "by means of a telecommunications device knowingly makes, creates, or solicits, and initiates the transmission of, any comment, request, suggestion, proposal, image, or other communication which is obscene or indecent, knowing that the recipient of the communication is under 18 years of age, regardless of whether the maker of such communication placed the call or initiated the communication."[5] The measure was added as an amendment to the Telecommunications Act of the same year.

Prodded by conservative groups, senators who did not desire to be labeled as being in favor of "smut" passed the measure 84-16.

"In a congressional conference committee the language of the CDA survived several challenges, and it became law when President Clinton signed the Telecommunications Act on February 8, 1996," said a policy analysis of the measure conducted by the libertarian CATO Institute.[6]

Within weeks several groups had filed lawsuits challenging the law, "including the American Civil Liberties Union, solid blue-chip companies such as Microsoft and Apple, and the American Library Association."[7] The case made it all the way to the U.S. Supreme Court, and in *Reno v. American Civil Liberties Union*, the high court unanimously overturned the law, ruling it was too broad and could actually be used to undermine the First Amendment.

The high court's decision was not an endorsement of Internet pornography. Far from it. Rather, justices realized that an overly broad law like the CDA could be expanded in the future to include *any speech* or expression that someone found "indecent" or simply objectionable.

"In making its case for the CDA," says a policy analysis by the CATO Institute, a libertarian think tank, "the Department of Justice…argued that the public interest in controlling access by minors to indecent material outweighs the speculative harm to free speech. Yet we have seen repeatedly that content regulation lends itself to abuse by political interest groups and thereby imposes sharp disincentives on those who would air controversial opinions."[8]

That's an astute observation, given that, too frequently, such efforts to ban or curb speech are driven by partisan politics rather than a sincere attempt to protect innocents from libel, slander, or indecency, notes Floyd Abrams, one of the nation's top First Amendment lawyers.

"Sometimes we seem to end up with two First Amendments," Abrams, author of *Speaking Freely: Trials of the First Amendment*, said in a speech to the CATO Institute May 9, 2005. "Too often, both sides of the political debate show a willingness to protect only the speech they like because they want to see their own opinions protected."[9]

The next target: The Internet

Despite pledges by Obama and like-minded politicians currently in power not to regulate other forms of media, there are those who believe the attempt is right around the corner. They say this will be the Left's attempt to finally muzzle, once and for all, opposition in all the various forms of communication and media. The most likely target is the Internet because, besides talk radio, that is the venue where ideology that competes with the left-wing mainstream media is most successful—and flourishing.

In fact, President Obama's choice to lead the powerful Office of

Information and Regulatory Affairs is none other than Cass Sunstein, a radical Harvard law professor. Sunstein may best be known for his extreme views on animal rights, which place him firmly on the PETA fringe. However, Sunstein has also argued in favor of a Fairness Doctrine for the Internet, because, according to him, "A system of limitless individual choices, with respect to communications, is not necessarily in the interest of citizenship and self-government."[10] Thus, the man President Obama wants to review (and tinker with) all government rules and regulations thinks that too much free speech is bad thing.

WorldNetDaily.com founder and editor-in-chief, Joseph Farah, compares the re-imposition of a modern-day version of the "Fairness Doctrine" to the nation's punitive tax system.

"[T]hose who say they believe in 'fairness' in taxation have perverted this idea to establish the graduated tax that soaks the higher end of the scale while leaving nearly half the public paying nothing at all — or, as Barack Obama suggests, even receiving money seized from the wealthy," Farah writes in his November 20, 2008 column.[11] He argues that in this case, "fairness" would actually lead to "censorship" of competing voices and ideas.

"This so-called 'Fairness Doctrine' is designed to go after Limbaugh and Sean Hannity and Michael Savage and hundreds of other outspoken critics of the party in power. It is designed to silence them. It is designed to censor their speech, pure and simple. It is designed to shut off debate in this country. It is designed to permanently empower a ruling class by destroying the only meaningful national soapbox of opposition," Farah argues.[12]

And that will happen in every media venue, he says.

Others agree. Adam Thierer, writing in *City Journal*, says:

The Left has a much bigger target in its regulatory crosshairs: the Internet. Over the past few years, many of the same policymakers and activists who have long trumpeted the Fairness Doctrine have advocated that its rough equivalent apply to Internet service providers. And they've come up with another Orwellian term for the proposal: "net neutrality." In theory, net-neutrality regulation would ban Internet operators from treating some bits of online traffic or communications more favorably than others, whether for economic or political purposes. Proponents of net neutrality use the same kind of fantastic rhetoric to describe it that they once used for the Fairness Doctrine: it's a way to "save the Internet" from "media barons," they say, who're apparently hell-bent on controlling all our thoughts and activities.[13]

"It's thus not hard to imagine a network neutrality law as the first step toward a Web fairness doctrine, with government trying to micromanage traffic flows to secure 'equal treatment' of opposing viewpoints (read: making sure all those noisy right-wingers get put back in their place)," says Brian Anderson, also writing in *City Journal.* "European Union advisory bodies have already called for such a rule, potentially forcing all opinion sites viewable in Europe — from tiny blogs to big news organizations — to post opposing opinions or face fines. It's not primarily the telecoms and cable companies we should worry about as threats to Internet freedom. It's the government regulators. Should Democrats regain control of Congress, expect another drive to police the Web."[14]

In discussing the political element, Thierer says:

That liberals would support such a Fairness Doctrine for the Internet is no surprise — they have long favored government regulation of media and communications markets. What's shocking, however, is that some conservative and family groups have joined the net-neutrality regulatory crusade. For example, in [a recent editorial] in the Washington Post, Roberta Combs, president of the Christian Coalition of America, joins Nancy Keenan, president of NARAL Pro-Choice America, in calling for congressional investigation of purported censorship by wireless operators. Combs, who has vociferously argued for net-neutrality regulation for communications and Internet companies, is now stepping up those calls, claiming that private companies want to squelch speech over wired or wireless networks. "We're asking Congress to convene hearings on whether existing law is sufficient to guarantee the free flow of information and to protect against corporate censorship," Combs and Keenan write.[15]

The problem is, what a corporation is permitted to do is much different from what the government is permitted to do, when it comes to speech and expression. Appearing at a forum hosted by the Progress and Freedom Foundation in September 2007, Harvard law professor Laurence Tribe said that, in his opinion, those who would impose net neutrality regulations on First Amendment grounds fail to appreciate "the fundamental right of editorial discretion."

"For the government to tell that entity that it cannot exercise that right in a certain way, that it must allow the projection of what it doesn't want to include, is a violation of its First Amendment rights," said Tribe.

Tribe's view was at odds with an editorial published in the *New York Times* a few weeks after his panel appearance. The *Times* editorial criticized an action by Verizon Wireless, accusing the company of censoring political speech on one of its mobile services:

> Late last month, Verizon Wireless denied an application from NARAL Pro-Choice America, a reproductive rights group, for a "short code," a few numbers that a mobile phone user can use to subscribe to a particular source of text messages. Verizon said its policy was to refuse "issue oriented" text-messaging programs from any group that "seeks to promote an agenda or distribute content that, in its discretion, may be seen as controversial or unsavory to any of our users." The policy also said political candidates may be granted short codes if the content is, "in VZW's sole discretion, not issue-oriented or controversial in nature."[16]

It should be noted that the *Times*' description of NARAL as a "reproductive rights" group is itself Orwellian. NARAL is an organization that is nearly militant in its efforts to push for unrestricted abortion. With that distinction noted, it's easy to see why the *Times'* editorial staff was upset with Verizon's decision, and it begs the question: Would the *Times'* staff be so vehement in its opposition to the Verizon decision had the company refused the same request to a group that vehemently opposed *abortion*? Based on the *Times'* consistent support for far-left causes, the answer is, almost certainly, no. In fact, the *Times* likely would have supported Verizon's decision to bar a group opposed to abortion.

That said, Tribe's position is that a private company has a right to regulate what content it transmits—but the government does *not*.

"The principle that Tribe articulated would apply equally to the *New York Times'* editors if they decided, say, not to run an advertisement from the Ku Klux Klan," writes Thierer. "That's why it's particularly puzzling that the Times ended its editorial about the Verizon incident by arguing that 'freedom of speech must be guaranteed, right now, in a digital world just as it has been protected in a world of paper and ink.' Does the editorialist believe, then, that government should regulate what ads the *Times* may run in its own pages?

"The *Times* apparently needs to brush up on the First Amendment. It's certainly true that any government action restricting online speech in this fashion would be unconstitutional," he continues. "When *government* censors, it does so in a sweeping and coercive fashion, prohibiting the public, at least in theory, from seeing or hearing what it disapproves of and punishing those who evade the restrictions with fines, penalties, or even jail time. Not so for Verizon or any other private carrier, which have no power to censor sweepingly or coercively. A world of difference exists between a private company's exercising editorial discretion to transmit—or not transmit—certain messages or types of content and government efforts to censor."[17]

Thierer concludes: "This twisted theory of the First Amendment cannot support net neutrality regulation. The First Amendment was intended to protect us from tyrannical, coercive government power, not the silly mistakes of private companies. And a new Fairness Doctrine for the Internet would have the same chilling effect on the vibrant exchange of ideas — especially conservative ones — that the old Fairness Doctrine for broadcast TV and radio did."[18]

With talk radio and the Internet securely under their control, the ideologues of the far Left would have all but won their battle against those who dare to disagree with them. It should be said that ideologues of conservative and traditional values should never be allowed to completely control debate either. But it must be noted that, aside from a few misguided examples, primarily it is far-left "progressives" who are trying to stifle the voices of dissent.

And should these leftist politicians, who currently control Congress and the White House, succeed in forming a formidable, unholy alliance with conservative and traditional values censors on the right, the result would likely be the death of the Internet as we know it, or, as unfortunate inhabitants of other countries already experience it, whether they know it or not.

In Burma, for example, the government blocks all access to what it considers to be opposition websites, as well as all Web-based e-mail. China blocks all access to any website critical of the ruling communist party. The Chinese government also filters any Web content having to do with "democracy" or "freedom of speech." Libya, Iran, North Korea, Saudi Arabia, Belarus, The Maldives, Nepal, Tunisia, Turkmenistan, Uzbekistan and Vietnam, like Burma and China, all censor the Internet in similar fashion and have been deemed "enemies of the Internet" by the press freedom watchdog group, Reporters Without Borders. In Cuba, which is also classified an "enemy of the Internet," Castro's regime can't afford the price of sophisticated Internet censorship techniques, so it has essentially outlawed Internet usage for all citizens. Going online in Cuba is a rare privilege that requires special permission from the government.[19]

All of these nations have one thing in common. Their governments don't trust their citizens with knowledge and freedom of speech, so they censor as much as they can and outlaw the rest. Doubtless few Americans would be proud of a United States that came to resemble any of these roguish nations.

Chapter Ten
Christian 'Hate Speech'

"Radical Christianity is just as threatening as radical Islam in a country like America where we have separation of church and state."

—Rosie O'Donnell, during the September 12, 2006 broadcast of ABC's *The View*

"NO KING BUT King Jesus." That is a phrase used by revolutionaries in England in the mid-17th century, during Britain's own civil war, but later adopted by some colonials in the "New World" during the American Revolution.[1] According to one explanation, it reflected the desire of our Founding Fathers to keep houses of worship "free of taxation and regulation by government" because they felt churches "were essential to maintaining the kind of Christian culture necessary for a free society" in America.[2]

Our Founders believed pastors, priests, and rabbis ought to be free to say what they wished regarding politics and the issues of the day because of their obvious importance to their flocks and because political pressure was often exerted against churches. Maryland, for example, was originally settled by Catholics in the mid-1600s but that charter was eventually revoked around 1680, leaving the Church of England the only established, "official" church, and Catholicism persecuted. Most other early English colonies in the New World were equally intolerant of differing religious views.[3]

But the prevailing attitude of our Founders regarding this freedom disappeared in 1954, thanks to an influential U.S. senator and future American president.

U.S. Sen. Lyndon B. Johnson, a Democrat from Texas, was facing stiff opposition in his reelection bid from nonprofit Christian groups, "some of whom were speaking their minds freely from the pulpits," according to one analysis.[4] In retaliation, Johnson engineered an effort to insert language into Internal Revenue Service code that prohibited nonprofit organizations, including churches, from endorsing or opposing candidates for political office. In effect, he used the power of Congress, and the enforcement power of perhaps the federal government's most feared agency, to circumvent the First Amendment and silence his critics.

The "Johnson Amendment," now codified as part of 26 U.S.C. sec 501(c)(3), states that a tax-exempt organization may not "participate in, or intervene in (including the publishing or distributing of statements), any political campaign on behalf of (or in opposition to) any candidate for public office."[5]

This action "should have been seen as a clear infringement of the First Amendment back in 1954 but it wasn't," writes Joseph Farah. "And this most regrettable action has haunted America ever since."[6]

This law successfully destroyed the separation our Founders intended between church and state. It took away a church's right to free speech, unless, of course, a church was willing to lose its tax-exempt status.

I can personally attest to the detrimental effect the Johnson Amendment has had on free speech in religious institutions. In an effort to promote my best-selling book, *The Audacity of Deceit: Barack Obama's War on American Values*, during the 2008 presidential election, I sought to purchase advertising in Catholic diocesan newspapers. The ad neither endorsed nor condemned any candidate for elected office. Rather, the ad listed Obama's well-known positions on many issues pertaining to abortion, and also displayed professional, public polling results showing where the American public came down on those issues. Only two dioceses out of 194 ran my paid advertisement. Though the ad was deemed to be in accordance with Catholic teaching, nearly every diocese refused to run the ad for fear it was "too political."

Likewise, a good friend of mine in the Catholic diocese of Arlington requested permission to distribute materials that had been prepared by the National Right to Life Committee at his parish. He was prompted to action by a report he had read in that diocese's own newspaper saying that many Catholics had little or no knowledge about Barack Obama's extreme support of abortion. The materials were, of course, in accordance with Catholic Church teaching. The Chancellor of the Arlington diocese not only forbade my friend to distribute the educational material, but threatened him with "arrest for criminal trespass" if he did.

The most recent "violation" of this heinous act came in early 2008, Joseph Farah notes, when Wiley Drake, pastor of the First Southern Baptist Church in Buena Park, California, was alerted by the IRS that he was under investigation by the federal tax agency for endorsing GOP presidential contender and former Arkansas Gov. Mike Huckabee. The investigation was the result of a complaint filed against Drake and his church by the group Americans United for Separation of Church and State. The agency said Drake was in violation of the IRS code for using church letterhead and a church radio show to speak his mind about Huckabee. As a result, his church was threatened with losing its tax-exempt status.[7]

In a letter dated May 12, 2008, the IRS cleared Drake of any wrongdoing, saying, in part, that Drake's endorsement came from his personal e-mail account and was sent to personal acquaintances, and that "no church resources were utilized in preparing or sending the email."[8]

"Whether you agree with Wiley Drake or not," Farah writes, "he and his church have every right to take a position on who should be our next president without risking the church's tax status…Under the First Amendment, Congress has no power to stifle freedom of speech."[9]

He's absolutely right. And yet, believers in Christ remain under assault by federal regulators. Enter the FCC and Christian broadcasters.

Any rule changes by the Federal Communications Commission under the auspices of the Obama administration and left-wing Democrats in Congress for more "fairness" on the airwaves would devastate Christian broadcasters, Christian radio stations, networks, and programming.

Consider for a moment the implications to Christian programming if stations were required to allow, for example, supporters of abortion, gay rights, environmental rights, and same-sex marriage, not to mention Muslims, Hindus, and atheists, equal time opposite supporters of Christian theology and religious principles. The medium would die a quick death. No conscientious Christian network or radio station owner would ever permit someone to broadcast ideology that directly contradicts the traditional theology and viewpoints embodied in the Bible regarding God, Jesus Christ, His disciples, and prophets. Nor should they be forced to.

By the same token, can you imagine left-wing ideologues forcing, for instance, cable channels that cater to homosexuals to broadcast traditional family values programming? Shows that feature a husband and wife involved in a loving, caring, and monogamous relationship? Shows that illustrate the cultural degradation that results from morally bankrupt practices like abortion? You probably can't.

As part of new rules being considered by the FCC is a provision that puts broadcast license renewal in the hands of political appointees — people whose jobs are, without question, dependent on their connections and loyalty to the reigning Democratic Party and President Barack Obama.

"You can imagine how this would affect renewal of Christian broadcast licenses," writes Jeff White of *ChristianWebsite.com*. "Any station that broadcasts messages opposed to sinful lifestyles would surely lose their license in areas where liberals are in charge of approving their renewals."[10]

Another facet of left-of-center political ideology that is creeping into the realm of religious broadcasting is the debate over the environment—an issue that many on the Left argue and defend with the vengeance of religion. In fact, to many left-wing ideologues, environmental socialism *is* their religion.

One organization that is driving "faith-based environmentalism" is the National Religious Partnership for the Environment.

"NRPE has forged relationships with a diverse group of religious organizations, including the U.S. Catholic Conference, the National Council of Churches of Christ, the Coalition on the Environment and Jewish Life, and the Evangelical Environmental Network," writes Larry West, for *About.com*. "These organizations work with NRPE to develop environmental programs that mesh with their own varied spiritual teachings. For instance, some 135,000 congregations—counting Catholic parishes, synagogues, Protestant and Eastern Orthodox churches, and evangelic congregations—have been provided with resource kits on environmental issues, including sermons for clergy, lesson plans for Sunday school teachers, and even conservation tips for church and synagogue building managers."[11]

If you ever wondered about the bias of the Left, here is a classic example. Environmentalism is clearly a political issue; one of our recent former vice presidents, Al Gore, has made a good living traveling the globe (and, ostensibly, contributing to so-called global warming in the process) preaching the gospel about how humans are destroying Mother Earth. But such eco-extremism extends way beyond Gore's fanaticism. Environmental issues have very much crept into everyday lawmaking decisions. Eco-friendly policies definitely have a friend in Barack Obama and his far-left allies, like House Speaker Nancy Pelosi. And yet, eco-nonsense can be freely discussed within the confines of a house of worship—even officially supported and sanctioned—without fear of violating the Johnson Amendment and running afoul of the IRS.

As Vaclav Klaus, president of the Czech Republic, has noted:

> The largest threat to freedom, democracy, the market economy, and prosperity at the end of the 20th and at the beginning of the 21st century is no longer socialism. It is, instead, the ambitious, arrogant, unscrupulous ideology of environmentalism.[12]

But the moment the political message runs counter to left-wing ideology, *bam!* The offender gets slapped with an IRS investigation, threats of prosecution, and loss of tax-exempt status.

And there is no reason to believe this kind of double-standard hypocrisy won't be extended in an Obama administration. Religious broadcasters beware: you are now on notice that anything you say against the liberal, far-left Establishment can and will be used against you.

'Hate speech'

Besides pushing for a new "Fairness Doctrine" to kill counter-liberal Christian speech on the air, the anti-free expression coalition in the White House and Congress is attempting another tactic—to label Christian talk as "hate speech" and regulate it by law. Speaker of the House Nancy Pelosi has labeled conservative and Christian talk "hate radio."[13]

"It is ironic to note that while liberals and their homosexual allies have an absolutist view of the First Amendment and free speech when it comes to pornography, child porn, obscene speech, flag burning, etc., they are now willing to stifle freedom of speech under the guise of providing 'fairness' on the airwaves. Other leftists are more honest: They admit they want to kick conservative and Christian talk show hosts off the air altogether in order to suppress what they view as 'hate speech,'" writes Andrea S. Lafferty, executive director of the Traditional Values Coalition.

She notes that Martin Firestone, a Democrat Party operative during the Kennedy-Johnson era, "reported to the Democratic National Committee that 'right-wingers operate on a strictly cash basis and it is for this reason that they are carried by so many small stations. Were our efforts to be continued on a year-round basis, we would find that many of these stations would consider the broadcasts of these programs bothersome and burdensome (especially if they are ultimately required to give us free time) and would start dropping the programs from their broadcast schedule.' He later said: 'Perhaps in the light of Watergate, our tactics were too aggressive, but we were up against ultra-right preachers who were saying vicious things about Kennedy and Johnson.'"

According to the nonprofit American Center for Law and Justice, the Fairness Doctrine "would have a significant and serious impact on Christian broadcasting."[14]

Jay Sekulow, chief counsel for the ACLJ, describes how the doctrine would put Christian broadcasters between a rock and a hard place, and, ultimately, out of business:

> In essence, the Federal Communications Commission (FCC) would be given the authority to require equal time to contrary positions on controversial issues. As you can imagine, the proclamation of the Gospel, the definition of marriage and the issue of abortion would all be deemed "controversial topics." Under this blatant form of compelled speech, broadcasters who air "Jay Sekulow Live!" or "Focus on the Family with Dr. Dobson" could be compelled to run a counter-viewpoint to the positions we just advocated. Therefore, Christian broadcasters would be put in the uncomfortable position of having to air positions that violate their conscience and sincerely held religious beliefs.[15]

Lafferty makes a dour prediction: Under an Obama administration, "Any criticism of liberal dogma or homosexuality will be condemned as 'hate speech' and forced from the airwaves."[16]

Dr. Frank Wright, President and CEO of the National Religious Broadcasters, correctly points out that a reenactment of the Fairness Doctrine would not only infringe on our right to freedom of speech and press, but also freedom of *religion*.

According to Wright:

> In today's cultural environment, traditional or "orthodox" religious teachings are increasingly the subject of controversy and would be regulated by the government under a restored fairness doctrine. Conventional Jewish and Christian teachings relating to such matters as sexual morality, marriage, parental responsibility, and the sanctity of human life are now hotly contested by an increasingly secularized society. In this environment, reinstitution of the fairness doctrine would lead to an unconstitutional "entanglement" of government regulators in religious matters and unconstitutionally infringe on the freedom of religion.[17]

Keenly aware of this mounting threat, the NRB Board of Directors passed a resolution in 2007, stating that the organization "strongly opposes any attempt to reinstate or make the 'Fairness Doctrine' the law of the land and further pledges to vigorously oppose any such action."[18]

NRB has a right to be concerned, having observed draconian anti-free speech "hate speech" laws wreaking havoc in other countries.

For example, in Canada it is a crime to commit "hate speech" against anyone based on their race, color, religion, ethnic origin, gender, or sexual orientation. Even Bible verses that speak against homosexuality can be considered criminal, as one unfortunate Canadian discovered.

In 2001, a Saskatchewan man and newspaper were found guilty of hate speech when they ran a newspaper ad that included Bible verses that addressed homosexuality. The man and the newspaper were forced to pay 1,500 Canadian dollars to each of three gay men who had filed the "hate speech" complaint.[19]

In Britain, a Saudi billionaire successfully sued an American author under British libel law, simply because the author exposed how the billionaire had financed terrorism. Britons have nothing that resembles U.S. First Amendment rights. The British court found the woman guilty, not because what she had written was untrue, but because it was liberally construed as libel, and ordered her to pay $225,000 to the billionaire.[20]

In Sweden in 2004, a Pentecostal minister was convicted of violating that country's hate speech laws for speaking out against homosexuality during a sermon. In 2005, the Swedish Supreme Court acquitted the minister;[21] however, the lower court's decision put others on notice that their right to speak freely does not exist.

In Australia in 2004, a Christian minister who was an expert on Islam was charged with "religious vilification" by the state of Victoria and found guilty of violating Australia's hate speech laws. His crime? Describing the specifics of that religion. Ironically, the man had fled Pakistan years earlier to save his own life when the university where he worked pressured him to become a Muslim. Under Pakistan's blasphemy law, his refusal could have subjected him to the death penalty.[22]

Not surprisingly, leftists often label viewpoints that differ from theirs as "hate speech." Given their penchant for name-calling, it is clear they would utilize any new Fairness Doctrine-type of legislation to kill whatever ideology didn't march in lockstep with their own. And, as Lafferty, Farah, and Sekulow have predicted, that ideology would soon be forced off the air.

Chapter Eleven
What Congress Will Attempt to Do

"The American people love a fair fight, especially where the issues of the day are debated. In a free market, fairness should be determined based upon equal opportunity, not equal results. As some voices are calling for Congress to enforce their idea of 'fairness' upon the American people, it would be good for us to proceed with caution whenever some would achieve their 'fairness' by limiting the freedom of others."

—Congressman Mike Pence (R-IN)

IN A PERFECT WORLD, governing documents would be perfectly understood, accepted, and implemented by those responsible for putting them into practice. In a perfect world, ambiguity would be nonexistent and all issues easily decided.

We don't live in a perfect world—far from it. Yet there are times when the path forward is crystal clear, and this is the case with the Fairness Doctrine. Quite simply, based on our U.S. Constitution as well as decades of practical experience, it's obvious such Fairness Doctrine mandates are neither legal, practical, nor appropriate for a society built upon guarded liberty.

The attempt to regulate speech or, more precisely, the methods by which people communicate, is nothing new. England's King Henry VIII in the early 1500s tried to control that new medium, the printing press, shortly after it was introduced, by requiring each press to be licensed. In addition, foreign books could be distributed only by the King's Stationer. Next, the Crown attempted to ban unlicensed books but found it could not.[1]

The Crown's attempts to control communication likely influenced our Founding Fathers to adopt, as the very First Amendment to our own Constitution, a rock-solid measure prohibiting any — *any* — government infringement on speech or expression, no matter the medium.

Over the course of our nation's history, however, it has become obvious that the First Amendment is not being applied with equal vigor over all forms of media.

"The language of the First Amendment does not distinguish one medium of speech from any other," says a congressional analysis by the CATO Institute. "Despite that, the Supreme Court has held that broadcasters should receive less protection than the print media. And broadcasters, like the print media under Henry VIII, are licensed. (Editor's note: Can you imagine our government ever forcing U.S. print media to be licensed?) The federal government's control over broadcasters' economic fortunes is easily leveraged into content controls. It is time to end this state of affairs."[2]

In recent years a number of censorship advocates have come before Congress to attempt to persuade it that banning speech — or, at a minimum, regulating it over the airwaves and Internet — is somehow both constitutional and necessary for the preservation of the Union. Neither argument is true, but censorship advocates continue to forge ahead anyway.

Fairness Doctrine advocates focus primarily on broadcasters because this is the medium they will attack first. Clamoring for more regulation, they say that broadcasters should be subject to more restrictive government oversight because they use public property — the airwaves. Yet, as First Amendment proponents point out, so do people who speak in public parks, college campuses, and numerous other venues considered "public property." And while such speakers are often required to get a license to use the venue they seek, they are free to say what they choose — even if that speech is highly offensive to many people.

Even newspapers, CATO points out, are delivered using public streets, and are "printed on paper made from trees that grew on federal lands."[3] As far as Washington's ownership of electronic mediums, there is not one shred of evidence that government can efficiently, effectively and, more important, *fairly*, run any sort of enterprise, let alone the broadcast medium. "Government ownership of the [electronic] spectrum is inefficient and unnecessary," says CATO.[4]

Right now, the Federal Communications Commission has control over content that is broadcast on what it, the federal government and federal courts, have long described as the "public" airwaves — on traditional radio and broadcast television stations and networks. In controlling the content, the FCC is, often arbitrarily, deciding what is and is not "indecent." Indecent material is defined as that which is "patently offensive," but that can mean different things to different people.

"D.C. Circuit Court of Appeals Judge Patricia Wald found that the definition could include programs on childbirth, AIDS, abortion, or almost any aspect of human sexuality," says CATO's analysis. "The FCC has admitted that it cannot describe exactly what material is 'indecent,' explaining that indecency rulings must be made on a 'case-by-case basis.' In other words, something is indecent if it offends a majority of FCC commissioners."[5]

Even the reliably left-wing American Civil Liberties Union gets it right. "Decades of experience have shown that the FCC's effort to regulate 'indecent' speech on the airwaves is arbitrary, inconsistent, and unpredictable. No government agency should be given such power under the Constitution," said Steven R. Shapiro, the group's legal director, in an August 7, 2008 "Friend of the Court" brief in the case of *FCC v. Fox Television Stations, Inc.*[6]

If such parameters were placed on newspapers and magazines, their owners would revolt en masse. They would fight back with successive lawsuits. They would rail against the imposition of any type of Fairness Doctrine on every editorial page, at every turn. And, according to the language and spirit of the First Amendment, they would be absolutely right to do so.

But broadcast radio and television stations don't have the luxury of protest. They know that they are at the economic mercy of the FCC, even today. They know that as long as an arbitrary federal agency controls their licensure, the agency controls their existence. If they want to renew their license or try to gain further access to the broadcast spectrum, they must play by the agency's rules. Under a new Fairness Doctrine, things will only get worse.

What Congress should do

Based on the history and culture of politics in our nation's capital, the hardest thing to do is to admit a mistake. But giving the FCC the arbitrary power it currently has was wrong. Moreover, it is definitely wrong to give the agency *more* power in the form of a new Fairness Doctrine that is even broader in scope than the one jettisoned by President Reagan's FCC over 20 years ago.

Since its creation via the Communications Act of 1934 the FCC has undergone a series of changes, but for the most part the agency has retained incredible influence over broadcasters—more, or less, depending on which political appointee was running the shop at the time. In the early 1940s, when the world was embroiled in global conflict for the second time in less than 50 years, the FCC actually went so far as to forbid broadcasters to editorialize.[8] Then, of course, from 1949 to 1987 the doctrine was imposed on radio and television stations, which, plainly, chilled free speech and limited a broadcaster's earning power.

But since the doctrine's removal, "there has been a stunning increase in the amount of informational programming on radio and television," says CATO.[9]

The recession of 2008-09 notwithstanding, the best thing Congress can do for the broadcast medium is to privatize it. Only then will the airwaves be free from an overarching federal agency, with its threats of economic retaliation and the loss of licensure and ability to operate. In essence, bring the concept of private property rights to the so-called "public" airwaves. Newspapers and periodicals operate free from federal licensure and so should radio and television broadcasters. Just as King Henry VIII sought to control the press by licensing its operation, the FCC currently controls talk radio in the same manner. It is impossible for anyone to truly speak freely with the sword of Damocles hanging over his head.

Though the current cry in Washington among the ruling Left is to foist more, not fewer, regulations on Americans, lawmakers would do well to cut the regulatory burdens faced by broadcasters. What could be more patriotic than expanding and strengthening the right of *all* Americans to speak freely?

Reasonable limits

Even if you're not a football fan, you may recall an incident that occurred at a halftime performance during Super Bowl XXXVIII, when pop star Justin Timberlake ripped off part of Janet Jackson's costume, exposing her right breast. The FCC received over 542,000 complaints, and any calls to deregulate the airwaves after that were immediately stifled. Chairman Michael K. Powell declared the incident outrageous and called it a "classless, crass and deplorable stunt." The agency levied a $550,000 fine on CBS and began to get much tougher on subsequent incidents of indecency.

One need not take a purely libertarian point of view and say there should be no limits whatsoever on network broadcasters. Programs like

115

the Super Bowl and others that are broadcast to children as well as adults can have some very black and white parameters—no nudity being one of them. Parents shouldn't have to worry about their kids being exposed to filth while watching certain shows.

Even if one did take the purely libertarian standpoint and say there should be no decency standards for broadcast radio and television, a good argument can be made that it would not result in the apocalypse. For example, there are a number of private and nonprofit media watchdog organizations that stand at the ready to give a well-publicized black eye to networks that offend common decency. CBS didn't gain popularity for what happened with the infamous "wardrobe malfunction." It lost popularity and spent months doing public relations damage control. As this experience showed, even if a network did decide to slouch toward Gomorrah, its "slouch" would only increase public demand for wholesome programming and other networks likely would step in to fill the void. Remember, network executives and station owners care about one thing: revenue. Even an atheist homosexual station owner would broadcast Christian religious programming if it was all he could do to keep his enterprise afloat.

The advent of new Fairness Doctrine-type legislation would only facilitate political censorship of talk radio and the Internet under the same old accusations of controversy, violence, offensive content, harmfulness to children, hate speech, and so on.

What is it, incidentally, that these self-appointed guardians of liberal morality are so adamant about protecting children *from*? Think of all the battles they fought against prayer in public schools, at football games, and at graduation ceremonies while indoctrination into the risky homosexual lifestyle was slipped quietly into the classroom with nary an objection, and the answer becomes clear.

In fact, the networks themselves have displayed an interesting interpretation of what is "offensive" and what is not. For example, in 2006, NBC clipped a segment of a popular children's show, *Veggie Tales*, because one of the characters mentioned God's love for children.[10] In 2002, ABC bleeped the word "Jesus" from the West Coast broadcast of its popular daily show, *The View*. One of the show's hosts was simply exclaiming thanks to Jesus for her success with a weight loss program.[11]

It's plain to see that, although the enemies of free speech may use "sensitivity" or "the children" as an excuse for their censorship, their real motivation is stifling debate and muzzling the opposition.

Congress is the only entity that can guarantee that the First Amendment remains intact. Although the courts all too frequently have shown a willingness to allow free speech and expression to be abused, that is often because Congress has failed to act and federal agencies have been left to their own politically appointed devices.

President Obama and the anti-free speech radicals within his administration and in the House and Senate cannot, by themselves, silence their critics. They must have the approval of the majority of lawmakers, and, by default, the quiet assent of the American people. We know this, because no sooner than the Left regained control of Congress following the 2006 elections, the Fairness Doctrine was resurrected. Although it was soundly defeated at that time, the Heritage Foundation points out that the victory may be short: "[T]he real battle over media regulation is still to come, and it won't involve the words 'Fairness Doctrine.'"[12]

We already know what supporters of censorship plan to do if they get their way. The Heritage Foundation has outlined the following potential policy changes:

• Strengthened limits on how many radio stations one firm can own, locally and nationally, as well as quotas for minority-owned stations;

• Shortened broadcast license terms from eight years to as few as three or two years;

• Requirement for radio broadcasters to regularly show they are operating in the "public interest." This would place radio stations at the mercy of local review boards that would decide whether or not a personality like Rush Limbaugh reflects the views of the "community at large";

• Imposition of "fees" on broadcasters who fail to meet these "public interest obligations." These "fees," actually fines, because they are punitive, would be used to support the liberal and already funded Corporation for Public Broadcasting.[13]

All of these measures are aimed at reducing the influence of competing ideologies. They will all be proposed under some form of new "comprehensive media reform" measure. But, as the Heritage Foundation warns, that measure won't contain the words "Fairness Doctrine."

"Limiting ownership...will eliminate many of the owners who favor conservative causes," writes James L. Gattuso, senior research fellow in regulatory policy at the Heritage Foundation.[14] "Public interest requirements can be defined almost any way a regulator wants—up to and perhaps even beyond that required by the old Fairness Doctrine. And the proposed fee provides regulators with a quite effective stick to compel compliance—as well as to direct funds to more ideologically compatible public broadcasters."

As for content that may be objectionable to certain elements of our society, namely our families, nowhere does the Constitution authorize the government to usurp the role of parents, whose right and responsibility it is to supervise what their kids are watching and listening to.

"We can best set an example for children by showing them that the First Amendment is much more than a bothersome obstacle to government, to be gotten around by indirect threats and economic pressure," says a CATO analysis.[15]

"We need less government, not more," writes Bobby Eberle of *GOPUSA.com*, "and politically motivated efforts by left-wing politicians to force the media to carry programs that fit their agenda is about as un-American as it gets. The government should stay out of the free speech business. The American people are the ultimate judges of what succeeds and what fails on the airwaves."[16]

That's good advice.

Chapter Twelve
What the FCC Could Do

"Economic growth requires innovation. Trouble is, Washington is practically designed to resist it. Built into the DNA of the most important agencies created to protect innovation, is an almost irresistible urge to protect the most powerful instead. The FCC is a perfect example...

"With so much in its reach, the FCC has become the target of enormous campaigns for influence. Its commissioners are meant to be 'expert' and 'independent,' but they've never really been expert, and are now openly embracing the political role they play...

"The solution here is not tinkering. You can't fix DNA. You have to bury it. President Obama should get Congress to shut down the FCC and similar vestigial regulators, which put stability and special interests above the public good."

—Lawrence Lessig, Stanford Law Professor, author and columnist

O NE OF THE PRIVILEGES of being president is getting to appoint your lieutenants. While some of those appointments, such as Cabinet-level posts, must be approved by the Senate, others—like the various federal department head positions—are solely up to the president.

The Federal Communications Commission is one such government agency whose top official will serve solely at the pleasure of President Obama. Obama's FCC chief was originally expected to be Henry Rivera, a telecommunications lawyer with the Washington, D.C. firm Wiley Rein. Rivera, a Democrat, previously served as a commissioner from 1981-1985 under FCC Chairman Mark Fowler.[1] In November 2008, shortly after reports surfaced that he was Obama's likely choice, Rivera was asked if he supported reinstating the Fairness Doctrine. He declined comment.

Brian Maloney of the blog "The Radio Equalizer" writes that Rivera "is expected to lead the push to dismantle commercial talk radio that is favored by a number of Democratic Party senators. Rivera will play a pivotal role in preventing critics from having a public voice during Obama's tenure in office."[2]

In mid-November 2008, Obama appointed Rivera to help his transition team review the FCC, "to aid the new administration in its planning decisions," CNET reported.[3] After a public outcry against his appointment to the FCC transition team, most notably because of his anti-free speech stance, Rivera was reassigned elsewhere by the Obama camp.

As of this writing, it is apparent that Obama will now nominate his old Harvard Law School friend, Julius Genachowski, to head the FCC. Genachowski was the mastermind behind the Obama campaign's online fundraising machine.

This would not be Genachowski's first stint with the FCC, as he served as counsel to President Bill Clinton's FCC Chairman Reed Hundt. Prior to that, Genachowski was a law clerk for Supreme Court Justice David Souter. He also served as a Legislative Assistant and Press Secretary to then-U.S. Rep. Charles Schumer (D-NY).

While at the FCC, Genachowski did some admirable work helping to repeal the outdated and burdensome fin-syn requirements. However, his current positions on two critical issues are cause for alarm.

Genachowski supports so-called "net neutrality" regulations, which, as discussed earlier in this book, are really the first step toward a Fairness Doctrine for the Internet. "Net neutrality" proponents like Genachowski would have government decide what content Internet operators and network owners must provide. Incredibly, they claim this is to keep the Internet free and open to all, when in reality, their goal is to usher the heavy hands of federal regulators into the tent. True champions of an open and free Internet understand that "net neutrality" laws are a solution in search of a problem—and when government regulators are given editorial authority over what private operators must provide, First Amendment rights are lost and "unfairness" becomes the name of the game.

Genachowski also advocates creating new media ownership rules that promote a diversity of voices on the airwaves.[4] In fact, Genachowski is credited with helping craft the Obama technology agenda, which states: "Encourage diversity in the ownership of broadcast media, promote the development of new media outlets for expression of diverse viewpoints, and clarify the public interest obligations of broadcasters who occupy the nation's spectrum."[5]

Such language is bureaucratese for "Fairness Doctrine." So-called "public interest" requirements would put broadcasters at the mercy of local review boards. Such boards would, of course, be politically charged entities with the power to bar any broadcast content that is not deemed to be in the "public interest" of the local community.

For those who ask, "What's wrong with making radio serve the public interest and the interest of individual localities?" consider the following.

If a radio station, whose principle market is an urban area that leans to the political left (like San Francisco, Detroit, Chicago, New York, or Philadelphia, to name a few), was forced to answer to an advisory committee made up of officials from that community, the committee might likely consider Rush Limbaugh, Sean Hannity, Glenn Beck, Mark Levin, and other conservative broadcasters as "not serving the local public interest."

As a result, that radio station might be forced to drop "controversial" hosts in those major cities, forcing those hosts to sell advertising that would not broadcast to those major city marketplaces. This, quite obviously, would close a lot of economic doors and force many popular radio hosts off the air. This is the danger of thousands of radio stations having "public interest" boards (which may be better named "commissar committees") that lay down the law when far-left voting populations are "offended" by what they hear.

Remember, in the election, Obama lost 2,245 U.S. counties, and only won 868 counties. Radio Stations in those 2,245 counties might be the first target for an FCC commissar committee.

Nothing we've seen from Genachowski indicates that he would oppose such an idea. Quite the contrary, his "diversity" and "public interest" language is the same used by those bureaucrats who would impose such a draconian system—bureaucrats like Obama-appointed interim FCC Chairman Michael Copps.

In a February 2009 interview with CNSNews.com, Copps said, "[W]e have to find a way to make radio reflect the public interest...I'm going to look at how we put public interest considerations and guidelines back into licensing for full power stations. I think that's something we need."[6]

In other words, Obama's interim chairman would hold the Sword of Damocles over the heads of station owners, by threatening to not renew their licenses unless they meet the public interest requirements concocted by Obama and the FCC. According to Copps, "mindless deregulation"[7] has hurt localism and diversity.

"If markets cannot produce what society really cares about," says Copps, "like a media that reflects the true diversity and spirit of our country, then government has a legitimate role to play."[8]

Like President Obama, Michael Copps and Julius Genachowski claim to have no desire to resurrect the Fairness Doctrine. This is disingenuous at best. Through localism, diversity, and public interest mandates, they aim to resurrect the very same, heavy-handed censorship that the Fairness Doctrine wrought—they just don't want to trip any alarm bells by calling it a "Fairness Doctrine."

Given the wretched and bleak history of the broadcasting industry during the dark days when the Fairness Doctrine was still in effect, what the FCC should avoid doing, at all costs, is becoming a politically partisan tool used to stifle dissent and kill debate. To do so would not only be a blatant violation of the letter, spirit, and intent of the First Amendment, it would be a serious blow to one of our founding cornerstones of liberty.

In the final year of the Bush administration, FCC Chairman Kevin Martin assured Americans that his agency was not considering a reinstatement of the doctrine. In a letter to Rep. Mike Pence (R-IN) in the summer of 2007, Martin said his agency had found "no compelling public interest to revisit its 1987 decision" overturning the doctrine, according to an Associated Press report. The report also said that Pence, in a letter to Martin, had expressed concern that the FCC might consider a new Fairness Doctrine after a number of "Democratic lawmakers suggested that Congress take another look at [it] after conservative talk radio show hosts aggressively attacked an immigration reform bill when it was on the Senate floor, contributing to its defeat".[9]

In his letter to Pence, Martin pointed out that government wasn't needed to ensure sufficient public access to a wide range of opinion. "Indeed," he wrote, "with the continued proliferation of additional sources of information and programming, including satellite broadcasting and the Internet, the need for the Fairness Doctrine has lessened even further since 1987."[10]

Martin's absolutely right. There is an amazing abundance of voices today—on the air, in print, online—to satisfy every point of view. There are liberal, conservative, libertarian, populist, and moderate voices; there are voices advocating the widest possible range of ideals on every major (and not-so-major) issue facing our country. And while some venues may not be as friendly to certain points of view as others, the fact that there are easily accessible ways to hear or read opposing viewpoints is undeniable. Therefore, there is no reason why the FCC should ever reimpose an outmoded, outdated regulatory blanket on free speech...*unless, of course, they want to use their agency as a political mallet to smash the opposition.*

"A breathtaking abundance of new and old media outlets for obtaining news, information, and entertainment exist today," says a news release for *A Manifesto for Media Freedom*, a book by Adam Thierer and Brian Anderson. "However, this media cornucopia is under threat from regulations meant to establish fairness, localism, diversity or other lofty ideals which, in practice, would lead to a much less varied and open media universe."[11]

Reimposing any sort of Fairness Doctrine—no matter what it's actually called—"would be a disaster, a kind of soft or not-so-soft tyranny that would wipe out whole sectors of media, curtailing free speech and impoverishing our democracy," the authors conclude.[12]

Currently the mission of the FCC, according to its website, is overly broad. Its role is to act as "an independent government agency" that is "charged with regulating interstate and international communications by radio, television, wire, satellite and cable."[13] There are about a dozen offices within the FCC—the Enforcement Bureau, the Media Bureau, Public Safety and Homeland Security Bureau, and Wireless Communications, to name just a few. Each has a role in ensuring, basically, that the FCC enforces all provisions of the Communications Act.

Not included in the agency's list of functions is enforcement of regulations mandating that opposing points of view be shown, broadcast, or depicted during news or editorial content broadcasts.

If President Obama is really serious about keeping liberty intact and encouraging free and open debate—so that, in these trying times, the best ideas and the most qualified people can be heard and understood, and so that the best decisions can be made about our nation's future—he will do everything in his power to keep the Fairness Doctrine, or anything like it, at bay.

Unfortunately, with the appointment of Genachowski to chair

the FCC, we can expect the agency to launch an assault on the First
Amendment, the likes of which has not been seen since the dark days of
the Fairness Doctrine. Specifically, we can expect the FCC to:

1. Shorten broadcast license terms from eight years to three or two years.
This would give the agency much more leverage in censoring what stations
air—it's one thing if station owners don't have to worry about renewing
their license for eight years in the future, but it's another thing if their renewal
is just around the corner.

2. Limit the number of stations one entity can own, both on a local and
national basis.

3. Establish a quota system for minority owned stations.

4. Impose draconian "localism" requirements and subject stations to the
review of local community boards whose members will decide whether or
not a station is airing content that is in the interest of the community. (Think
of what a San Francisco community board would do to a local station that
airs Rush Limbaugh.)

Whether in the Oval Office or on the nation's airwaves, smart
people with good ideas deserve a fair hearing. Doing the right thing
for the country at the right time is not an accident and it should not be
handicapped by partisanship.

The fact is the American people expect their elected leaders to
preserve and protect their freedoms, as much as they deserve to hear
all sides of an issue. Leaders at every level need to hear from everyone
involved in helping make decisions if they are to decide on the best
course of action.

If a new Fairness Doctrine is reimposed on the nation's broadcasters,
debate will suffer, our Constitution will be weakened, and the tyrants
will win. Even if a new "Fairness Doctrine" isn't imposed, Obama's

FCC could still institute a number of rule changes (listed above) that would have the net effect of Fairness Doctrine-style censorship.

Responsible FCC commissioners, no matter their political appointment or point of view, should jealously guard the gates of freedom by opposing any new attempt to regulate speech.

During his campaign for president, Obama made a point of emphasizing his zeal for free speech and open debate. However, if Obama supports the reimposition of the Fairness Doctrine in any form, or by any other name, and if he instructs his hand-picked FCC Commission to enforce heavy-handed policies that regulate content over the airwaves, his broken promise to seek open and spirited debate, as well as his dripping contempt for the Constitution and liberty, will become clear.

And our nation will have been harmed, perhaps irreparably.

Chapter Thirteen
Meet the Enemies of Ben Franklin and Thomas Paine

"Without Freedom of Thought there can be no such Thing as Wisdom; and no such Thing as Public Liberty, without Freedom of Speech…

"This sacred Privilege is so essential to free Governments, that the Security of Property, and the Freedom of Speech always go together; and in those wretched Countries where a Man cannot call his Tongue his own, he can scarce call any Thing else his own. Whoever would overthrow the Liberty of a Nation, must begin by subduing the Freeness of Speech; a Thing terrible to Publick Traytors."

—Benjamin Franklin, writing as "Silence Dogood" to the author of the *New-England Courant*, No. 8, July, 9 1722

"If journalism and the rest of the country have forgotten [Thomas] Paine, why should we remember another of history's lost souls?

"Because we owe Paine. He is our dead and silenced ancestor. He made us possible…

"Paine's odyssey made him the greatest media figure of his time, one of the unseen but profound influencers of ours. He made more noise in the information world than any messenger or pilgrim before or since…

"If the old media (newspapers, magazines, radio, and television) have abandoned their father, the new media (computers, cable, and the Internet) can and should adopt him. If the press has lost contact with its spiritual and ideological roots, the new media culture can claim them as its own.

"For Paine does have a legacy, a place where his values prosper and are validated millions of times a day: the Internet. There, his ideas about communications, media ethics, the universal connections between people, and the free flow of honest opinion are all relevant again, visible every time one modem shakes hands with another."

—Jon Katz, Journalist, Author, and former Executive Producer of *CBS Morning News*, writing in the May 1995 issue of *Wired* magazine

T HERE CAN BE NO DOUBT that the people below, consciously or not, are enemies of the First Amendment freedoms that Ben Franklin so vehemently defended, and Thomas Paine so effectively utilized to foster the American Revolution. These are the people who would destroy the freedom of speech, limit media freedom, and make tyranny possible.

President Barack Obama

"Senator Obama supports media-ownership caps, network neutrality, public broadcasting, as well as increasing minority ownership of broadcasting and print outlets."

—President-elect Barack Obama's Press Secretary, Michael Ortiz, June 2008

House Speaker Nancy Pelosi

Human Events Political Editor John Gizzi to House Speaker Nancy Pelosi (D-CA): *"Do you personally support revival of the Fairness Doctrine?"*

House Speaker Nancy Pelosi: *"Yes."*

— June 24, 2008, at a breakfast hosted by the *Christian Science Monitor* in Washington, D.C.

House Majority Leader Steny Hoyer

"There is a real concern about the monopoly of information and the skewering of information that the American public gets."

—House Majority Leader Steny Hoyer telling *CNSNews.com* that he would support reactivating the Fairness Doctrine to "ensure the availability of fair and balanced information to the American public." *CNSNews.com*, July 31, 2008

Cass Sunstein, Director of President Obama's Office of Information and Regulatory Affairs

"A system of limitless individual choices, with respect to communications, is not necessarily

in the interest of citizenship and self-government."

—President Obama's Regulatory Czar, Cass Sunstein, arguing that a Fairness Doctrine is needed for the Internet, in his book, *Republic.com 2.0*

Former President Bill Clinton

"Well, you either ought to have the Fairness Doctrine or we ought to have more balance on the other side."

—Former President Bill Clinton, in an interview with liberal radio show host Mario Solis Marich, February 12, 2009

Senate Majority Leader Harry Reid

"[The political landscape is] still not as good as it would have been had we not had everything consolidated, and the Fairness Doctrine [had not gone] out the window, and all the things that were so 'fair.'"

—Senate Majority Leader Harry Reid (D-NV) in a 2006 interview with *Salon.com*

Assistant Senate Majority Leader Dick Durbin

"It's time to reinstitute the Fairness Doctrine. I have this old-fashioned attitude that when Americans hear both sides of the story, they're in a better position to make a decision."

—Sen. Dick Durbin (D-IL), *The Hill*, 2007

Sen. Charles Schumer

"I think we should all be fair and balanced, don't you? The very same people who don't want the Fairness Doctrine want the FCC to limit pornography on the air. I am for that... But you can't say government hands off in one area to a commercial enterprise but you are allowed to intervene in another. That's not consistent."

—Sen. Charles Schumer (D-NY), *Fox News*, November 4, 2008

Sen. Dianne Feinstein

"I believe very strongly that the airwaves are public and people use these airwaves for profit.

But there is a responsibility to see that both sides and not just one side of the big public questions of debate of the day are aired and are aired with some modicum of fairness."

—Sen. Dianne Feinstein (D-CA)

Sen. John Kerry

"I think the fairness doctrine ought to be there, and I also think equal time doctrine ought to come back."

—Sen. John Kerry (D-MA), June 26, 2007, on WNYC's *Brian Lehrer Show*

Sen. Debbie Stabenow

BILL PRESS: *Yeah, I mean, look: They have a right to say that. They've got a right to express that. But, they should not be the only voices heard. So, is it time to bring back the Fairness Doctrine?*

SEN. DEBBIE STABENOW (D-MI): *I think it's absolutely time to pass a standard. Now, whether it's called the Fairness Standard, whether it's called something else — I absolutely think it's time to be bringing accountability to the airwaves. I mean, our new president has talked rightly about accountability and transparency. You know, that we all have to step up and be responsible. And, I think in this case, there needs to be some accountability and standards put in place.*

BILL PRESS: *Can we count on you to push for some hearings in the United States Senate this year, to bring these owners in and hold them accountable?*

SEN. DEBBIE STABENOW (D-MI): *I have already had some discussions with colleagues and, you know, I feel like that's gonna happen. Yep.*

—Sen. Debbie Stabenow (D-MI), as interviewed by liberal radio show host Bill Press, February 5, 2009

Sen. Tom Harkin

BILL PRESS: *And, thanks for your leadership, thanks for your good work, it's great to have you there Senator. And, great to have you on the show. Appreciate it.*

SEN. TOM HARKIN (D-IA): *Well, anytime—just let me know Bill. I love being with you, and thanks again for all you do to get the truth and the facts out there. By the way, I read your Op-Ed in the Washington Post the other day. I ripped it out, I took it into my office and said 'there you go, we gotta get the Fairness Doctrine back in law again.'*

BILL PRESS: *Alright, well good for you. You know, we gotta work on that, because they are just shutting down progressive talk from one city after another. All we want is, you know, some balance on the airwaves, that's all. You know, we're not going to take any of the conservative voices off the airwaves, but just make sure that there are a few progressives and liberals out there, right?*

SEN. TOM HARKIN (D-IA): *Exactly, and that's why we need the fair—that's why we need the Fairness Doctrine back.*

BILL PRESS: *We'll work on that together. Hey, thanks, Senator! Always good to talk to you.*

—Sen. Tom Harkin (D-IA), as interviewed by liberal radio show host Bill Press, February 11, 2009

Rep. Anna Eshoo

"I'll work on bringing [the Fairness Doctrine] back. I still believe in it."

—Rep. Anna Eshoo, speaking to the Palo Alto *Daily Post*, December 2008

Rep. Maurice Hinchey

"The FCC has abandoned its responsibility to protect the public interest. Starting with the Reagan Administration's elimination of the Fairness Doctrine and culminating with the establishment this week of the Powell Rules, big media corporations and their allies have succeeded in gradually pushing aside the public interest in favor of big profits."

—Rep. Maurice Hinchey (D-NY), in a June 2003 press release trumpeting his bill, "The Reclaiming the Public's Airwaves Act," which would have reinstated the Fairness Doctrine

Rep. Louise Slaughter

"I have [been fighting to resurrect the Fairness Doctrine]. And, you know, I was so committed to it and I kept doing bills. Because the airwaves belong to the people...

"[Rush Limbaugh] doesn't make any pretense of being a news person or even telling you the truth. He says he's an entertainer. [He is] dominating America and a waste of good broadcast time and a waste of our airwaves...

"I'm concerned about television as well. But radio is probably where we're going to get the biggest problems in trying to get this done, because people have the radio on all day. They listen to it. And I think that says a lot. I think we can see that reflected in what people are thinking and feeling today."

—Rep. Louise Slaughter (D-NY) in a December 2004 interview with Bill Moyers, speaking in support of her bill, "The MEDIA Act," which would have reinstated the Fairness Doctrine

FAIR (Fairness and Accuracy in Reporting)

"As a guarantor of balance and inclusion, the Fairness Doctrine was no panacea. It was somewhat vague, and depended on the vigilance of listeners and viewers to notice imbalance. But its value, beyond the occasional remedies it provided, was in its codification of the principle that broadcasters had a responsibility to present a range of views on controversial issues."

—Steve Rendall, senior analyst for the pro-Fairness Doctrine group FAIR (Fairness and Accuracy in Reporting. Among other things, FAIR is also busy trying to dispel the "myth" of pro-Obama media bias

The Center for American Progress

"The disparities between conservative and progressive programming reflect the absence of localism in American radio markets. This shortfall results from the consolidation of ownership in radio stations and the corresponding dominance of syndicated programming operating in economies of scale that do not match the local needs of all communities.

"This analysis suggests that any effort to encourage more responsive and balanced radio programming will first require steps to increase localism and diversify radio station ownership to better meet local and community needs. We suggest three ways to accomplish this:

• Restore local and national caps on the ownership of commercial radio stations.

• Ensure greater local accountability over radio licensing.

• Require commercial owners who fail to abide by enforceable public interest obligations to pay a fee to support public broadcasting."

—John Halpin, James Heidbreder, Mark Lloyd, Paul Woodhull, Ben Scott, Josh Silver, S. Derek Turner, in a June 2007 report authored for *The Center for American Progress and Free Press*, arguing for greater regulation of the airwaves

The 41 U.S. senators who, in an effort to smear talk radio, dishonestly accused Rush Limbaugh of degrading American servicemen and women. (Even after they were proven wrong, and their letter was proven to be a lie, they refused to apologize):

Blanche Lincoln (AR)	*Barbara Boxer (CA)*
Dianne Feinstein (CA)	*Ken Salazar (CO)*
Christopher Dodd (CT)	*Joseph Biden (DE)*
Tom Carper (DE)	*Bill Nelson (FL)*
Daniel Akaka (HI)	*Daniel Inouye (HI)*
Tom Harkin (IA)	*Richard Durbin (IL)*
Barack Obama (IL)	*Mary Landrieu (LA)*
Edward M. Kennedy (MA)	*John Kerry (MA)*
Benjamin Cardin (MD)	*Barbara Mikulski (MD)*
Carl Levin (MI)	*Debbie Stabenow (MI)*
Amy Klobuchar (MN)	*Max Baucus (MT)*

Jon Tester (MT)

Byron Dorgan (ND)

Bob Menendez (NJ)

Hillary Rodham Clinton (NY)

Sherrod Brown (OH)

Bob Casey (PA)

Sheldon Whitehouse (RI)

Patrick Leahy (VT)

Patty Murray (WA)

Jay Rockefeller (WV)

Kent Conrad (ND)

Frank Lautenberg (NJ)

Harry Reid (NV)

Charles Schumer (NY)

Ron Wyden (OR)

Jack Reed (RI)

Jim Webb (VA)

Bernie Sanders (VT)

Robert Byrd (WV)

The 115 members of Congress who voted against Rep. Mike Pence's (R–IN) amendment to a general appropriations bill that prohibited the FCC from using any funds to implement the Fairness Doctrine for one year (the moratorium expired September 30, 2008):

Marion Berry (AR)

Ed Pastor (AZ)

Lois Capps (CA)

Anna Eshoo (CA)

Bob Filner (CA)

Mike Honda (CA)

Zoe Lofgren (CA)

Jerry McNerney (CA)

Linda Sánchez (CA)

Adam Schiff (CA)

Pete Stark (CA)

Raul Grijalva (AZ)

Xavier Becerra (CA)

Susan Davis (CA)

Sam Farr (CA)

Jane Harman (CA)

Barbara Lee (CA)

Doris Matsui (CA)

George Miller (CA)

Loretta Sanchez (CA)

Hilda Solis (CA)

Ellen Tauscher (CA)

Maxine Waters (CA)

Lynn Woolsey (CA)

Rosa DeLauro (CT)

Ron Klein (FL)

Robert Wexler (FL)

Henry Johnson (GA)

Mazie Hirono (HI)

Bruce Braley (IA)

Danny Davis (IL)

Jesse Jackson, Jr. (IL)

Nancy Boyda (KS) No longer serving

William Jefferson (LA) No longer serving

Ed Markey (MA)

Martin Meehan (MA) No longer serving

John Olver (MA)

Albert Wynn (MD) No longer serving

Tom Allen (ME) No longer serving

John Dingell (MI)

Sander Levin (MI)

Betty McCollum (MN)

Emanuel Cleaver (MO)

G.K. Butterfield (NC)

Mel Watt (NC)

Rush Holt (NJ)

Bill Pascrell (NJ)

Shelley Berkley (NV)

Michael Arcuri (NY)

John Hall (NY)

Maurice Hinchey (NY)

Carolyn Maloney (NY)

Diane Watson (CA)

Mike Thompson (CA)

John Larson (CT)

Debbie W. Schultz (FL)

Sanford Bishop (GA)

John Lewis (GA)

Leonard Boswell (IA)

David Loebsack (IA)

Luis Gutierrez (IL)

Jan Schakowsky (IL)

Michael Capuano (MA

Barney Frank (MA)

James McGovern (MA)

Richard Neal (MA)

Steny Hoyer (MD)

Chris Van Hollen (MD)

John Conyers (MI)

Carolyn Kilpatrick (MI)

Keith Ellison (MN)

William Clay, Jr. (MO)

Bennie Thompson (MS)

Tom Price (NC)

Paul Hodes (NH)

Frank Pallone (NJ)

Donald Payne (NJ)

Gary Ackerman (NY)

Yvette Clarke (NY)

Brian Higgins (NY)

Nita Lowey (NY)

Jerrold Nadler (NY)

Charles Rangel (NY)

Edolphus Towns (NY)

Stephanie Tubbs Jones (OH) Deceased

Dennis Kucinich (OH)

Earl Blumenauer (OR)

David Wu (OR)

Christopher Carney (PA)

Chaka Fattah (PA)

John Murtha (PA)

Patrick Kennedy (RI)

Lloyd Doggett (TX)

Al Green (TX)

Jim Moran (VA)

Peter Welch (VT)

Rick Larsen (WA)

Tammy Baldwin (WI)

Louise Slaughter (NY)

Nydia Velázquez (NY)

Marcy Kaptur (OH)

Betty Sutton (OH)

Peter DeFazio (OR)

Robert Brady (PA)

Mike Doyle (PA)

Paul Kanjorski (PA)

Joe Sestak (PA)

Jim Langevin (RI)

Charlie Gonzalez (TX)

Eddie Bernice Johnson (TX)

Bobby Scott (VA)

Brian Baird (WA)

Jim McDermott (WA)

Gwen Moore (WI)

The 113 members of Congress who voted in favor of Rep. Pence's amendment to a general appropriations bill, which prohibited the FCC from using any funds to implement the Fairness Doctrine for one year (the moratorium expired September 30, 2008), BUT REFUSED to sign a discharge petition that would have released The Broadcaster Freedom Act from committee and allowed for an up-or-down vote on the Act in the House. The Broadcaster Freedom Act, authored by Rep. Pence, would prohibit the Federal Communications Commission from ever reinstating the Fairness Doctrine.

Robert Cramer (AL) No longer serving

Mike Ross (AR)

Gabrielle Giffords (AZ)

Artur Davis (AL)

Vic Snyder (AR)

Harry Mitchell (AZ)

Joe Baca (CA)

Howard Berman (CA)

Dennis Cardoza (CA)

Jim Costa (CA)

Grace Napolitano (CA)

Lucille Roybal-Allard (CA)

Brad Sherman (CA)

Diana DeGette (CO)

Ed Perlmutter (CO)

John Salazar (CO)

Mark Udall (CO)

Joe Courtney (CT)

Christopher Murphy (CT)

Eleanor Holmes Norton (DC)

Allen Boyd (FL)

Corrine Brown (FL)

Kathy Castor (FL)

Alcee Hastings (FL)

Tim Mahoney (FL) No longer serving

Kendrick Meek (FL)

John Barrow (GA)

Jim Marshall (GA)

David Scott (GA)

Madeleine Bordallo (Guam)

Melissa Bean (IL)

Jerry Costello (IL)

Rahm Emanuel (IL)

Phil Hare (IL)

Daniel Lipinski (IL)

Bobby Rush (IL)

André Carson (IN)

Joe Donnelly (IN)

Brad Ellsworth (IN)

Baron Hill (IN)

Peter Visclosky (IN)

Dennis Moore (KS)

Ben Chandler (KY)

John Yarmuth (KY)

Charlie Melancon (LA)

William Delahunt (MA)

Stephen Lynch (MA)

Elijah Cummings (MD)

Dutch Ruppersberger (MD)

John Sarbanes (MD)

Michael Michaud (ME)

Dale Kildee (MI)

Bart Stupak (MI)

James Oberstar (MN)

Collin Peterson (MN)

Timothy Walz (MN)

Russ Carnahan (MO)

Ike Skelton (MO)

Gene Taylor (MS)

Bob Etheridge (NC)

Mike McIntyre (NC)

Brad Miller (NC)

Heath Shuler (NC)

Earl Pomeroy (ND)

Carol Shea-Porter (NH)

Robert Andrews (NJ)

Steven Rothman (NJ)	*Albio Sires (NJ)*
Tom Udall (NM)	*Joseph Crowley (NY)*
Eliot Engel (NY)	*Kirsten Gillibrand (NY)*
Steve Israel (NY)	*Carolyn McCarthy (NY)*
Gregory Meeks (NY)	*José Serrano (NY)*
Anthony Weiner (NY)	*Tim Ryan (OH)*
Zach Space (OH)	*Charles Wilson (OH)*
Darlene Hooley (OR) No longer serving	*Dan Boren (OK)*
Jason Altmire (PA)	*Tim Holden (PA)*
Patrick Murphy (PA)	*Allyson Schwartz (PA)*
Eni Faleomavaega (Samoa)	*John Spratt (SC)*
Stephanie Herseth Sandlin (SD)	*Jim Cooper (TN)*
Lincoln Davis (TN)	*Bart Gordon (TN)*
John Tanner (TN)	*Henry Cuellar (TX)*
Chet Edwards (TX)	*Gene Green (TX)*
Sheila Jackson Lee (TX)	*Silvestre Reyes (TX)*
Nick Lampson (TX) No longer serving	*Ciro Rodriguez (TX)*
Jim Matheson (UT)	*Rick Boucher (VA)*
Donna Christian-Christensen (VI)	*Norman Dicks (WA)*
Jay Inslee (WA)	*Adam Smith (WA)*
Steve Kagen (WI)	*Ron Kind (WI)*
David Obey (WI)	*Shelley Moore Capito (WV)*
Alan Mollohan (WV)	*Nick Rahall (WV)*

If your congressman or senators appear in this chapter as proponents of censorship, call them and let them know that you *DISAPPROVE* of their efforts to censor talk radio, trample the First Amendment, and threaten your right to free speech! Simply call the Capitol Hill Switchboard at 202-224-3121 and ask for your congressman or senator by name.

Chapter Fourteen
Meet the Guardians of Free Speech

"I do not agree with what you have to say, but I'll defend to the death your right to say it."

—Voltaire

THE CONGRESSMEN, SENATORS, POLICY GROUPS and columnists in this chapter are not merely passive supporters of our First Amendment rights—rather, they have taken real action to stop the reinstatement of the Fairness Doctrine. As such, they deserve thanks and support from free speech advocates.

Congressional Vanguard

Far-left pundits and bloggers would have us believe that conservatives and free speech advocates are using the Fairness Doctrine controversy as a straw man to win support from a broad cross-section of American voters. That claim is absurd, given the strong words of the Democratic leadership in Congress in support of reinstating the Fairness Doctrine. The fact that half of the Republican caucus in each House of Congress has co-sponsored legislation to prevent the FCC from reinstating the Fairness Doctrine suggests that the threat is very real.

Left-wingers in Congress began their current push to reinstate the Fairness Doctrine in 2007. In response, Sen. Norm Coleman (R-MN) introduced an amendment to a defense appropriations bill to prohibit any funds in the bill from being used to adopt a fairness rule. Unfortunately, Senate Democrats blocked that amendment. Thirty-five Senate Republicans signed on as co-sponsors of Coleman's Broadcaster

Freedom Act of 2007 (S. 1748) while another eight co-sponsors signed on to Sen. John Thune's (R-SD) bill (S. 1742) that would have prohibited the FCC from promulgating new Fairness Doctrine rules.

The 35 co-sponsors of the Broadcaster Freedom Act of 2007:

Jeff Sessions (AL)	*Jon Kyl (AZ)*
John McCain (AZ)	*Wayne Allard (CO)*
Mel Martinez (FL)	*Saxby Chambliss (GA)*
Johnny Isakson (GA)	*Larry E. Craig (ID)*
Mike Crapo (ID)	*Richard G. Lugar (IN)*
Pat Roberts (KS)	*Sam Brownback (KS)*
Jim Bunning (KY)	*Mitch McConnell (KY)*
David Vitter (LA)	*Christopher S. Bond (MO)*
Thad Cochran (MS)	*Roger F. Wicker (MS)*
Elizabeth Dole (NC)	*Chuck Hagel (NE)*
Judd Gregg (NH)	*John Ensign (NV)*
George V. Voinovich (OH)	*Tom Coburn (OK)*
James M. Inhofe (OK)	*Jim DeMint (SC)*
Lindsey Graham (SC)	*John Thune (SD)*
Lamar Alexander (TN)	*Bob Corker (TN)*
John Cornyn (TX)	*Kay Bailey Hutchison (TX)*
Robert F. Bennett (UT)	*John Barrasso (WY)*
Michael B. Enzi (WY)	

The eight co-sponsors of S. 1742, a bill that would have barred the FCC from repromulgating the Fairness Doctrine:

John McCain (AZ)	*Wayne Allard (CO)*

Larry Craig (ID)

Jim Bunning (KY)

George Voinovich (OH)

Richard Lugar (IN)

Mitch McConnell (KY)

Michael Enzi (WY)

In the House of Representatives, Congressman Mike Pence (R-IN) sponsored a companion to Thune's bill. Pence's effort drew the following 208 co-sponsors in the previous Congress:

Don Young (AK)

Spencer Bachus (AL)

Terry Everett (AL)

John Boozman (AR)

Trent Franks (AZ)

John B. Shadegg (AZ)

Mary Bono Mack (CA)

John Campbell (CA)

David Dreier (CA)

Wally Herger (CA)

Darrell E. Issa (CA)

Daniel E. Lungren (CA)

Buck McKeon (CA)

Devin Nunes (CA)

Dana Rohrabacher (CA)

Doug Lamborn (CO)

Thomas G. Tancredo (CO)

Michael N. Castle (DE)

Ginny Brown-Waite (FL)

Ander Crenshaw (FL)

Mario Diaz-Balart (FL)

Robert B. Aderholt (AL)

Jo Bonner (AL)

Mike D. Rogers (AL)

Jeff Flake (AZ)

Rick Renzi (AZ)

Brian P. Bilbray (CA)

Ken Calvert (CA)

John T. Doolittle (CA)

Elton Gallegly (CA)

Duncan Hunter (CA)

Jerry Lewis (CA)

Kevin McCarthy (CA)

Gary G. Miller (CA)

George Radanovich (CA)

Edward R. Royce (CA)

Marilyn N. Musgrave (CO)

Christopher Shays (CT)

Gus M. Bilirakis (FL)

Vern Buchanan (FL)

Lincoln Diaz-Balart (FL)

Tom Feeney (FL)

Ric Keller (FL)

Connie Mack (FL)

John L. Mica (FL)

Jeff Miller (FL)

Adam Putnam (FL)

Ileana Ros-Lehtinen (FL)

Cliff Stearns (FL)

Dave Weldon (FL)

C.W. Bill Young (FL)

Paul C. Broun (GA)

Nathan Deal (GA)

Phil Gingrey (GA)

Jack Kingston (GA)

John Linder (GA)

Tom Price (GA)

Lynn A. Westmoreland (GA)

Steve King (IA)

Tom Latham (IA)

Bill Sali (ID)

Michael K. Simpson (ID)

Judy Biggert (IL)

Dennis J. Hastert (IL)

Timothy V. Johnson (IL)

Mark Steven Kirk (IL)

Ray LaHood (IL)

Donald Manzullo (IL)

Peter J. Roskam (IL)

John Shimkus (IL)

Jerry Weller (IL)

Dan Burton (IN)

Steve Buyer (IN)

Mark E. Souder (IN)

Jerry Moran (KS)

Todd Tiahrt (KS)

Geoff Davis (KY)

Ron Lewis (KY)

Harold Rogers (KY)

Ed Whitfield (KY)

John A. Yarmuth (KY)

Rodney Alexander (LA)

Richard H. Baker (LA)

Charles W. Boustany Jr. (LA)

Bobby Jindal (LA)

Jim McCrery (LA)

Steve Scalise (LA)

Roscoe G. Bartlett (MD)

Wayne T. Gilchrest (MD)

Dave Camp (MI)

Vernon J. Ehlers (MI)

Peter Hoekstra (MI)

Joe Knollenberg (MI)

Thaddeus G. McCotter (MI)

Candice S. Miller (MI)

Mike J. Rogers (MI)

Fred Upton (MI)

Timothy Walberg (MI)

Michele Bachmann (MN)

John Kline (MN)

Jim Ramstad (MN)

W. Todd Akin (MO)

Roy Blunt (MO)

Sam Graves (MO)

Charles W. Pickering (MS)

Dennis R. Rehberg (MT)

Virginia Foxx (NC)

Walter B. Jones Jr. (NC)

Mike McIntyre (NC)

Jeff Fortenberry (NE)

Lee Terry (NE)

Rodney P. Frelinghuysen (NJ)

Frank A. LoBiondo (NJ)

Christopher H. Smith (NJ)

Heather Wilson (NM)

Jon Porter (NV)

Peter T. King (NY)

John M. McHugh (NY)

James T. Walsh (NY)

Steve Chabot (OH)

David L. Hobson, (OH)

Steven C. LaTourette (OH)

Deborah Pryce (OH)

Jean Schmidt (OH)

Michael R. Turner (OH)

Mary Fallin (OK)

John Sullivan (OK)

Jason Altmire (PA)

Phil English (PA)

Tim Murphy (PA)

Joseph R. Pitts (PA)

Bill Shuster (PA)

Jo Ann Emerson (MO)

Kenny C. Hulshof (MO)

Roger F. Wicker (MS)

Howard Coble (NC)

Robin Hayes (NC)

Patrick T. McHenry (NC)

Sue Wilkins Myrick (NC)

Adrian Smith (NE)

Mike Ferguson (NJ)

Scott Garrett (NJ)

Jim Saxton (NJ)

Stevan Pearce (NM)

Dean Heller (NV)

Vito Fossella (NY)

John R. "Randy" Kuhl (NY)

Thomas M. Reynolds (NY)

John A. Boehner (OH)

Paul E. Gillmor (OH)

Jim Jordan (OH)

Robert E. Latta (OH)

Ralph Regula (OH)

Patrick J. Tiberi (OH)

Tom Cole (OK)

Frank D. Lucas (OK)

Greg Walden (OR)

Charles W. Dent (PA)

Jim Gerlach (PA)

John E. Peterson (PA)

Todd Russell Platts (PA)

Luis G. Fortuño (PR)

J. Gresham Barrett (SC)

Bob Inglis (SC)

Marsha Blackburn (TN)

John J. Duncan Jr. (TN)

Joe Barton (TX)

Michael C. Burgess (TX)

Michael Conaway (TX)

Louie Gohmert (TX)

Ralph Hall (TX)

Sam Johnson (TX)

Michael T. McCaul (TX)

Ron Paul (TX)

Pete Sessions (TX)

Mac Thornberry (TX)

Chris Cannon (UT)

Jo Ann Davis (VA)

Thelma D. Drake (VA)

Virgil H. Goode Jr. (VA)

Robert J. Wittman (VA)

Doc Hastings (WA)

David G. Reichert (WA)

Paul Ryan (WI)

Shelley Moore Capito (WV)

Henry E. Brown Jr. (SC)

Joe Wilson (SC)

David Davis (TN)

Zach Wamp (TN)

Kevin Brady (TX)

John R. Carter (TX)

John Abney Culberson (TX)

Kay Granger (TX)

Jeb Hensarling (TX)

Kenny Marchant (TX)

Randy Neugebauer (TX)

Ted Poe (TX)

Lamar Smith (TX)

Rob Bishop (UT)

Eric Cantor (VA)

Tom Davis (VA)

Randy J. Forbes (VA)

Bob Goodlatte (VA)

Frank Wolf (VA)

Cathy McMorris Rodgers (WA)

Thomas E. Petri (WI)

F. James Sensenbrenner Jr. (WI)

Barbara Cubin (WY)

Congressional Republicans, faced with an incoming Democratic administration and another Democratic-controlled Congress, wasted no time in reintroducing legislation to block the FCC from resurrecting the Fairness Doctrine. Congressman Mike Pence introduced H.R. 226 early in January 2009 and already has 164 co-sponsors. Over in the

Senate, Sen. Jim DeMint (R–SC) sponsored S. 34, a bill that would also prevent the FCC from reinstating the doctrine, and has garnered 28 co-sponsors. Also, Sen. Jim Inhofe (R–OK) sponsored S. 62, which shares the same intent as Sen. DeMint's legislation.

The 164 co-sponsors of H.R. 226:

Robert B. Aderholt (AL)	*Spencer Bachus (AL)*
Jo Bonner (AL)	*Mike D. Rogers (AL)*
John Boozman (AR)	*Jeff Flake (AZ)*
Trent Franks (AZ)	*John B. Shadegg (AZ)*
Brian P. Bilbray (CA)	*Mary Bono Mack (CA)*
Ken Calvert (CA)	*John Campbell (CA)*
David Dreier (CA)	*Elton Gallegly (CA)*
Wally Herger (CA)	*Duncan D. Hunter (CA)*
Darrell E. Issa (CA)	*Jerry Lewis (CA)*
Daniel E. Lungren (CA)	*Kevin McCarthy (CA)*
Howard P. "Buck" McKeon (CA)	*Tom McClintock (CA)*
Gary G. Miller (CA)	*George Radanovich (CA)*
Dana Rohrabacher (CA)	*Edward R. Royce (CA)*
Doug Lamborn (CO)	*Gus M. Bilirakis (FL)*
Ginny Brown-Waite (FL)	*Vern Buchanan (FL)*
Ander Crenshaw (FL)	*Lincoln Diaz-Balart (FL)*
Mario Diaz-Balart (FL)	*Connie Mack (FL)*
John L. Mica (FL)	*Jeff Miller (FL)*
Bill Posey (FL)	*Adam H. Putnam (FL)*
Thomas J. Rooney (FL)	*Cliff Stearns (FL)*
C.W. Bill Young (FL)	*Paul C. Broun (GA)*
Nathan Deal (GA)	*Phil Gingrey (GA)*
Jack Kingston (GA)	*John Linder (GA)*

Tom Price (GA)

Tom Latham (IA)

Judy Biggert (IL)

Mark Steven Kirk (IL)

Peter J. Roskam (IL)

John Shimkus (IL)

Steve Buyer (IN)

Lynn Jenkins (KS)

Todd Tiahrt (KS)

Brett Guthrie (KY)

John A. Yarmuth (KY)

Charles W. Boustany Jr. (LA)

Steve Scalise (LA)

Dave Camp (MI)

Peter Hoekstra (MI)

Candice S. Miller (MI)

Fred Upton (MI)

John Kline (MN)

Jo Ann Emerson (MO)

Roy Blunt (MO)

Howard Coble (NC)

Walter B. Jones Jr. (NC)

Mike McIntyre (NC)

Jeff Fortenberry (NE)

Lee Terry (NE)

Scott Garrett (NJ)

Christopher H. Smith (NJ)

Christopher J. Lee (NY)

Steve Austria (OH)

Jim Jordan (OH)

Lynn A. Westmoreland (GA)

Michael K. Simpson (ID)

Timothy V. Johnson (IL)

Donald A. Manzullo (IL)

Aaron Schock (IL)

Dan Burton (IN)

Mark E. Souder (IN)

Jerry Moran (KS)

Geoff Davis (KY)

Ed Whitfield (KY)

Rodney Alexander (LA)

John Fleming (LA)

Roscoe G. Bartlett (MD)

Vernon J. Ehlers (MI)

Thaddeus G. McCotter (MI)

Mike J. Rogers (MI)

Michele Bachmann (MN)

W. Todd Akin (MO)

Sam Graves (MO)

Denny Rehberg (MT)

Virginia Foxx (NC)

Patrick T. McHenry (NC)

Sue Wilkins Myrick (NC)

Adrian Smith (NE)

Rodney P. Frelinghuysen (NJ)

Frank A. LoBiondo (NJ)

Dean Heller (NV)

John M. McHugh (NY)

John A. Boehner (OH)

Robert E. Latta (OH)

Jean Schmidt (OH)

Michael R. Turner (OH)

Mary Fallin (OK)

John Sullivan (OK)

Jason Altmire (PA)

Jim Gerlach (PA)

Joseph R. Pitts (PA)

Bill Shuster (PA)

J. Gresham Barrett (SC)

Bob Inglis (SC)

Marsha Blackburn (TN)

David P. Roe (TN)

Joe Barton (TX)

Michael C. Burgess (TX)

Michael K. Conaway (TX)

Louie Gohmert (TX)

Ralph M. Hall (TX)

Sam Johnson (TX)

Michael T. McCaul (TX)

Ron Paul (TX)

Pete Sessions (TX)

Mac Thornberry (TX)

Jason Chaffetz (UT)

J. Randy Forbes (VA)

Robert J. Wittman (VA)

Doc Hastings (WA)

David G. Reichert (WA)

Paul Ryan (WI)

Shelley Moore Capito (WV)

Patrick J. Tiberi (OH)

Tom Cole (OK)

Frank D. Lucas (OK)

Greg Walden (OR)

Charles W. Dent (PA)

Tim Murphy (PA)

Todd Russell Platts (PA)

Glenn Thompson (PA)

Henry E. Brown Jr. (SC)

Joe Wilson (SC)

John J. Duncan Jr. (TN)

Zach Wamp (TN)

Kevin Brady (TX)

John R. Carter (TX)

John Abney Culberson (TX)

Kay Granger (TX)

Jeb Hensarling (TX)

Kenny Marchant (TX)

Randy Neugebauer (TX)

Ted Poe (TX)

Lamar Smith (TX)

Rob Bishop (UT)

Eric Cantor (VA)

Bob Goodlatte (VA)

Frank R. Wolf (VA)

Cathy McMorris Rodgers (WA)

Thomas E. Petri (WI)

F. James Sensenbrenner Jr. (WI)

Cynthia M. Lummis (WY)

The 28 co-sponsors of S. 34:

Jeff Sessions (AL)	*Jon Kyl (AZ)*
Mel Martinez (FL)	*Saxby Chambliss (GA)*
Johnny Isakson (GA)	*Mike Crapo (ID)*
Richard G. Lugar (IN)	*Sam Brownback (KS)*
Pat Roberts (KS)	*Mitch McConnell (KY)*
David Vitter (LA)	*Christopher S. Bond (MO)*
Thad Cochran (MS)	*Roger Wicker F. (MS)*
Richard Burr (NC)	*Mike Johanns (NE)*
John Ensign (NV)	*George V. Voinovich (OH)*
Tom Coburn (OK)	*James M. Inhofe (OK)*
Lindsey Graham (SC)	*John Thune (SD)*
Lamar Alexander (TN)	*Bob Corker (TN)*
John Cornyn (TX)	*Kay Bailey Hutchison (TX)*
John Barrasso (WY)	*Michael B. Enzi (WY)*

Public Policy Players

Conservative think tanks and policy organizations are well aware of the danger posed by the Fairness Doctrine, and several of them have taken specific action to combat this threat. Major efforts include:

• *The Media Research Center's Free Speech Alliance*

A project of Brent Bozell's Media Research Center, the Free Speech Alliance aims to mobilize 500,000 citizens to end the threat of the Fairness Doctrine and other attacks on Free Speech. The Alliance is right on the mark, as the coming congressional battle over the Fairness Doctrine is truly a small part of a larger discussion about free speech and the radical Left's goal to muzzle any opposing views. The Alliance already has the following 36 organizations on board and many of them are conservative heavyweights:

American Civil Rights Union

American Conservative Union

American Family Business Institute

American Service Council

American Shareholders Association

Americans for Prosperity

Americans for Tax Reform

Ax the Tax

Capital Research Center

Capitol Hill Prayer Alert

Center for Competitive Politics

Center for Freedom and Prosperity

Center for Individual Freedom

Center for Military Readiness

Competitive Enterprise Institute

Concerned Women for America

Council for Citizens Against Government Waste

Defenders of Liberty International

Discovery Institute

Family Research Council

Focus on the Family

Institute for Liberty

International Right to Life Federation

Jim Gilchrist and Minutemen American Defense

Let Freedom Ring

Life Issues Institute

Maj. Gen. Paul Vallely and Stand Up America USA
Media Freedom Project
National Religious Broadcasters
National Taxpayers Union
Property Rights Alliance
RightMarch.com
Salem Communications Corporation
Sam Adams Alliance
Sixty Plus
Star Parker and Urban CURE

• *The Media Research Center's Culture and Media Institute (CMI) (www.cultureandmediainstitute.org)*

The mission of the Culture and Media Institute is to preserve and help restore America's culture, character, traditional values, and morals against the assault of the liberal media elite, and to promote fair portrayal of social conservatives and religious believers in the media. In July 2008, CMI published the report, "Unmasking the Myths Behind the Fairness Doctrine," that debunked all the major arguments employed by censorship activists to resurrect the Fairness Doctrine.

• *National Rifle Association (www.nra.org)*

America's premiere defender of our Second Amendment rights is also a vigilant guardian our First Amendment rights. NRA helped lead the fight against the free speech-killing McCain-Feingold campaign finance "reform" bill. According to NRA Executive Vice President Wayne LaPierre: "The First Amendment is a not a right limited for a privileged few, for politicians and big media. It is the voice of the people, the man on the street. It is my voice, your voice." NRA has also been educating and activating its massive grassroots network to combat the Fairness Doctrine.

• *United Republican Fund (www.protectfairness.com)*

ProtectFairness.com is a project of the Illinois-based United Republican Fund. ProtectFairness.com is dedicated to building a national movement to stop the Fairness Doctrine and to safeguard the current environment of competing ideas on America's airwaves. This website enables visitors to sign a petition to Congress to stop the Fairness Doctrine and keeps visitors up to date on the latest news on the Fairness Doctrine fight.

• *Accuracy in Media (www.aim.org)*

Accuracy In Media (AIM) is a nonprofit, grassroots media watchdog that critiques inaccurate and biased news stories and sets the record straight on important issues that have received slanted coverage. AIM and its point man on the Fairness Doctrine, Cliff Kincaid, have been on the front lines over the past few years covering the Fairness Doctrine threat.

• *Center for Competitive Politics (www.campaignfreedom.com)*

The Center for Competitive Politics is a nonprofit organization founded in November 2005 by former FEC Chairman Bradley A. Smith and campaign finance attorney Stephen M. Hoersting. CCP's mission, through legal briefs, studies, historical and constitutional analyses, and media communication, is to educate the public on the actual effects of money in politics and the results of a freer and more competitive electoral process. CCP has begun to focus on the Fairness Doctrine given the threat it poses to political talk over the airwaves.

• *American Radio Free Speech (www.americanradiofreespeech.org)*

This newly formed nonprofit organization serves as a clearinghouse for information on what friends and enemies of free speech are doing. The site also contains contact information for those seeking to get in touch with other organizations involved in the Fairness Doctrine battle. American Radio Free Speech is funded by a grant, but it does accept donations under $5 to help cover the expense of sending eight e-mails on behalf of site visitors when legislation is moving. One e-mail goes out to the visitor's U.S. representative, one to each of the visitor's two U.S. senators, and one to each of the five FCC commissioners.

These e-mails will be sent out pending any immediate action on the Fairness Doctrine by Congress or the FCC. The website also contains the names and contact info for all senators and representatives who favor censorship of talk radio.

• *The Heritage Foundation (www.heritage.org)*

One of the oldest and most respected conservative think tanks, the Heritage Foundation is an important resource for Hill Republicans. Over the past several years Heritage has published a number of valuable issue briefs on the Fairness Doctrine and its threat to our First Amendment rights.

• *The Cato Institute (www.cato.org)*

CATO is the libertarian nonprofit public research organization equivalent to the Heritage Foundation. Like the Heritage Foundation, the CATO Institute is a major public policy player in the Fairness Doctrine fight, and has published numerous articles and analyses that expose how the doctrine would undermine the First Amendment.

• *Free Congress Foundation (www.freecongress.org)*

Up until his death in December 2008, Free Congress Foundation founder Paul Weyrich was among the most vocal leaders rallying free speech advocates against the Fairness Doctrine. Weyrich frequently wrote on the topic and helped sound the alarm on Capitol Hill through his powerful network and influential weekly meetings with conservative leaders and members of Congress. Even in death, his leadership on this issue continues to inspire.

• *The American Conservative Union (www.conservative.org)*

The American Conservative Union (ACU) is the nation's oldest and largest grassroots conservative lobbying organization. ACU has also been engaged in the Fairness Doctrine fight and has produced a number of excellent editorials on the subject.

• *The American Center for Law and Justice (www.aclj.org)*

The Washington, D.C.-based American Center for Law and Justice (ACLJ) focuses on constitutional law and is specifically dedicated to the ideal that religious freedom and freedom of speech are inalienable, God-given rights. The Center's purpose is to ensure that those rights are protected under the law, and to that end, ACLJ has been a vigilant guardian of free speech. ACLJ's Chief Counsel Jay Sekulow is a vocal opponent of the Fairness Doctrine.

• *Family Research Council (www.frc.org)*

The Family Research Council has rallied against censorship and consistently urges its supporters to back Rep. Mike Pence's efforts to ban the FCC from bringing back the Fairness Doctrine. According to FRC President Tony Perkins: "Americans are entitled to the free exchange of ideas and an independent press that supports such an exchange. A vigorous national debate on issues of the day is one of the hallmarks of democracy."

• *Goldwater Institute (www.goldwaterinstitute.org)*

The Goldwater Institute champions the limited government, conservative values of its namesake, the late Sen. Barry Goldwater. As such, the Institute has been especially vigilant in the defense of Americans' right to free speech and firm in its opposition to the Fairness Doctrine.

• *National Association of Broadcasters (www.nab.org)*

The National Association of Broadcasters is a trade association that advocates on behalf of more than 8,300 free, local radio and television stations and also broadcast networks before Congress, the Federal Communications Commission and the Courts. The Association is on the frontlines fighting against any and all attempts to resurrect the Fairness Doctrine, and vigorously supports legislation, such as the Broadcaster Freedom Act, that is designed to protect broadcasters from censorship.

• *Radio Equalizer Blog (radioequalizer.blogspot.com)*

This blog spot, run by talk show host Brian Maloney, does an excellent job of keeping visitors up to date on the latest Fairness Doctrine information.

Vocal Support and Energized Punditry

Many columnists have lent their powerful voices to fight against censorship and the Fairness Doctrine. Space does not allow for listing all writers who have been especially vigilant in guarding our freedom of speech; however, below are a select few.

It is important to note that Fairness Doctrine opponents are not solely the providence of the political Right. Liberal talk executive and Air America founder *Jon Sinton* opposes the planned re-imposition of the old FCC policy. In his December 22, 2008 *Wall Street Journal* editorial, Stinton writes, "The Fairness Doctrine is an anachronistic policy that, with the abundance of choices on radio today, is entirely unnecessary." (http://online.wsj.com/article/SB122990390599425181.html) Sinton clearly understands the would-be reimposition of this policy for what it is — an infringement of free speech.

George Will, in his excellent column, "Reactionary Liberals Assault the Media," notes that "because liberals have been even less successful in competing with conservatives on talk radio than Detroit has been in competing with its rivals, liberals are seeking intellectual protectionism in the form of regulations that suppress ideological rivals."[1] (http://townhall.com/columnists/GeorgeWill/2008/12/07/reactionary_liberals_assault_the_media)

Tony Blankley points out in his column, "Liberals Leave the Watchtowers of Freedom," that "conservative opposition to liberalism at least has talk radio as a strong voice to our constituencies, and that has helped balance the advantage the liberals get from mainstream media bias... If they succeed [at reinstituting the Fairness Doctrine], they would come dangerously close to silencing their political opposition."[2] (http://townhall.com/columnists/TonyBlankley/2008/12/10/liberals_leave_the_watchtowers_of_freedom)

In his column, "Beware of the 'Fairness Doctrine,'" *William Rusher* writes, "What those who support the 'fairness doctrine' are really saying is that they don't enjoy the fact that their views have so little support. And while that's perfectly understandable, it is no justification for the proposition that society must artificially create a situation in which unpopular views receive the same attention and respect as others that have more."[3] **(http://townhall.com/columnists/WilliamRusher/2008/11/24/ beware_of_the_fairness_doctrine)**

Michael Barone writes in his column, "The Coming Obama Thugocracy," that "Today's liberals seem to be taking their marching orders from other quarters. Specifically, from the college and university campuses where administrators, armed with speech codes, have for years been disciplining and subjecting to sensitivity training any students who dare to utter thoughts that liberals find offensive. The campuses that used to pride themselves as zones of free expression are now the least free part of our society."[4] **(http://townhall.com/columnists/ MichaelBarone/2008/10/11/the_coming_obama_thugocracy)**

In one of the best columns on the subject, *David Limbaugh* aptly points out in his piece, "The Un-Fairness Doctrine: Unevening the Playing Field, by Law" that "different views are already heard—and not just in the mainstream media. There have never been more media choices. Nothing—except consumer resistance—precludes liberal entry into the talk radio market. But the First Amendment doesn't require people to listen to and support your message. Liberals had no interest in balance before the advent of conservative talk radio. They don't have any interest in balance now; indeed we're finally approaching a balance: new media versus old media. But to them "balance" means dominance, just like "bipartisanship" means Republican capitulation."[5] **(http://townhall.com/columnists/DavidLimbaugh/2007/01/19/ the_un-fairness_doctrine_unevening_the_playing_field,_by_law)**

Paul Greenberg puts an even finer point on the root of Speaker Pelosi's desire to resurrect the Fairness Doctrine. In his column, "The Unfairness Doctrine," Greenberg wrote: "They sigh for the good old days when riffraff like Rush Limbaugh and numerous imitators could be shut out of the public discourse. It is those who claim to speak for The People who resent it most when people choose to listen to somebody else."[6] (http://townhall.com/columnists/ PaulGreenberg/2008/10/17/the_unfairness_doctrine)

John Fund, in his column, "Fairness is Foul," provides some historical perspective on the Fairness Doctrine and its illegitimate roots: "But the Fairness Doctrine has always had fans in the corridors of power because it gave incumbents a way of muzzling their opponents. The Kennedy administration used it as a political weapon. Bill Ruder, Kennedy's assistant secretary of commerce, explained: 'Our strategy was to use the Fairness Doctrine to challenge and harass right-wing broadcasters and hope that the challenges would be so costly to them that they would be inhibited and decide it was too expensive to continue.'"

Fund continues: "Sen. Dianne Feinstein rails against 'one-sided programming' that has pushed the American people into 'extreme views without a lot of information.' She thinks Americans deserve to know 'both sides of the story.' Isn't it enough that National Public Radio, subsidized by the government, serves as a vehicle for liberal voices in just about every community in the country?"[7] (http://www.opinionjournal.com/diary/?id=110010795)

Joseph Farah, in his column, "Misunderstanding the 'Fairness Doctrine,'" puts the lie to any claims that such a policy could be a good thing for conservatives and libertarians, as it could force the major TV networks to air conservative content.

"There is no 'good news' for freedom-loving or even fairness-loving people in the so-called 'Fairness Doctrine,'" writes Farah. "It is a frontal assault on our Constitution. It is a blatant attack on the uniquely American institution of freedom of the press. It is an effort to squelch dissent against Big Government in the United States—pure and simple." [8] (http:// www.worldnetdaily.com/index.php/index.php?pageId=84807)

Finally, my late good friend and conservative icon *Paul Weyrich* penned a column just before he died that stated "[A]ll of us who believe in free speech must continue to be vigilant. 'Eternal vigilance is the price of liberty ...' and also the price of freedom of the airwaves. More than once in all my years in Washington I have seen a movement organize itself quietly and effectively and successfully. Well and good when it's a movement for freedom or another good cause. Wrecking talk shows by curbing their free speech is censorship and danger. Let us continue our vigilance." [9] (http:// townhall.com/columnists/PaulWeyrich/2008/10/22/illusion_or_ actuality_many_prominent_media_figures_and_democrats_oppose_ fairness_doctrine_re-imposition)

The simple truth is that Americans can ill-afford to allow a select few individuals who occupy the seats of power in Congress to trample our First Amendment rights in the name of so-called *fairness*. We should all aspire to be as vigilant in guarding our sacred right to free speech as the people and organizations above. Ultimately, this tremendous threat to liberty affects everyone, regardless of ideology, race, gender, or creed.

Get Involved!

Contact the following organizations and support their fight to keep the radio waves uncensored:

The Media Research Center's Free Speech Alliance
325 S. Patrick Street
Alexandria, VA 22314
703-683-9733
www.mrc.org/freespeechalliance/

The Media Research Center's Culture and Media Institute (CMI)
325 S. Patrick Street
Alexandria, VA 22314
703-683-9733
www.cultureandmediainstitute.org

National Rifle Association
11250 Waples Mill Road
Fairfax, VA 22030
1-800-672-3888
www.nra.org

United Republican Fund/ProtectFairness.com
100 West Monroe Street Suite 1600
C/O Morris, Rathnau & Dela Rosa
Chicago, IL 60603
www.protectfairness.com

Accuracy in Media

4455 Connecticut Avenue NW Suite #330
Washington, DC 20008
1-800-787-4567
www.aim.org

Center for Competitive Politics

124 West Street S., Suite 201
Alexandria, VA 22314
703-894-6800
www.campaignfreedom.org

American Radio Free Speech

www.americanradiofreespeech.org

The Heritage Foundation

214 Massachusetts Ave NE
Washington DC 20002-4999
202-546-4400
www.heritage.org

The Cato Institute

1000 Massachusetts Avenue NW
Washington D.C. 20001-5403
202-842-0200
www.cato.org

Free Congress Foundation

1423 Powhatan Street #2

Alexandria, VA 22314

703-837-0030

www.freecongress.org

The American Conservative Union

1007 Cameron Street

Alexandria, VA 22314

703-836-8602

www.conservative.org

The American Center for Law and Justice

P.O. Box 90555

Washington, DC 20090-0555

1-800-296-4529

www.aclj.org

Family Research Council

801 G Street NW

Washington, D.C. 20001

202-393-2100

www.frc.org

Goldwater Institute

500 E. Coronado Road

Phoenix, AZ 85004

602-462-5000

www.goldwaterinstitute.org

National Association of Broadcasters

1771 N Street NW
Washington, DC 20036
202-429-5300
www.nab.org

Radio Equalizer Blog

e-mail: radioequalizer@aol.com
http://radioequalizer.blogspot.com/

Fairness Doctrine Update

On February 26, 2009, just as this book was going to press, the U.S. Senate held two key votes concerning the Fairness Doctrine.

Sen. Jim DeMint (R-SC) offered an amendment to S. 160, the "District of Columbia House Voting Rights Act," to prevent the Federal Communications Commission from re-promulgating the Fairness Doctrine. DeMint's amendment passed overwhelmingly 87-11.

However, Sen. Dick Durbin (D-IL) offered another amendment to the same bill designed "to encourage and promote diversity in communication media ownership, and to ensure that the public airwaves are used in the public interest." This amendment passed 57-41.

As of this writing, S. 160, and both of the above amendments, have not yet become law.

Readers of this book know that the Durbin amendment is nothing more than a backdoor attempt to enact Fairness Doctrine-style censorship. The Durbin amendment is virtually identical to the language the Obama Administration uses when discussing censorship alternatives to the Fairness Doctrine.

Notes

Introduction

1. Congressman Steve King (R-IA), "Fairness Doctrine is Chinese-style Censorship," Press Release, December 17, 2008

2. Museum of Broadcast Communications, "Fairness Doctrine," accessed online at **http://www.museum.tv/archives/etv/F/htmlF/ fairnessdoct/fairnessdoct.htm**

3. Ibid

4. Ibid

5. Ibid

6. Definition from Merriam-Webster dictionary online at **http://www. merriam-webster.com/dictionary/fairness**

Chapter One: Left-wing Media Monopoly

1. Michael S. Malone, "Media's President Bias and Decline," *ABC News Online*, Nov. 11, 2008, accessed online at **http://abcnews.go.com/ print?id=6099188**

2. Ibid

3. Deborah Howell, "An Obama Tilt in Campaign Coverage," The *Washington Post*, Nov. 9, 2008

4. Ibid

5. Ibid

6. Jake Tapper, "Halperin Decries 'Disgusting' Pro-Obama Media Bias in Election Coverage," *ABCNews.com*, Tapper's blog, accessed online at http://blogs.abcnews.com/politicalpunch/2008/11/halperin-decrie.html

7. Ibid

8. Kevin Peters, "Can media bias affect an election?" *KHOU-TV* Web site, Nov. 4, 2008, accessed at http://www.khou.com/news/local/politics/stories/khou081104_tnt_media-bias-obama-mccain.17c44f584.html

9. "Voters Give Media Failing Grades in Objectivity for Election 2008," *Rasmussen Reports* survey, published June 8, 2008. Results accessed online at http://www.rasmussenreports.com/public_content/politics/election_20082/2008_presidential_election/voters_give_media_failing_grades_in_objectivity_for_election_2008

10. Ibid

11. Ibid

12. Malone, "Media's President Bias and Decline," *ABC News Online*

13. Ibid

14. Ibid

15. Ibid

16. "Oprah on Obama: 'I cried my eyelashes off,'" The *Associated Press* Aug. 29, 2008.

17. Lowell Ponte, "Oprah, Olbermann, and Media Bias," *Newsmax.com*, Sept. 8, 2008

18. "Oprah on Obama: 'I cried my eyelashes off,'" The *Associated Press*

19. Lowell Ponte, "Oprah, Olbermann, and Media Bias," *Newsmax.com*

20. Data provided by the *Media Research Center*, accessed at http://www.mrc.org/ on Nov. 26, 2008

21. Michael S. Malone, "Media's President Bias and Decline," *ABC News Online*

22. Ibid

23. Ibid

Chapter Two: The First Amendment Under Attack

1. Jim Meyers, "Schumer Compares Talk Radio to 'Pornography,'" *Newsmax.com*, November 4, 2008

2. Alexander Bolton, "GOP Preps for Talk Radio Confrontation," *The Hill*, June 27, 2007

3. Ibid

4. Ibid

5. First Amendment to the United States Constitution

6. John P. Foley, "The Jeffersonian Cyclopedia," *Funk and Wagnalls Company*, 1900, p. 717

7. Jonah Goldberg, "The Perils of Dan-nial," *National Review Online*, September 17, 2004

8. *Media Research Center,* "Rather Fails to Admit Forgery or Apologize for Impugning Critics," *CyberAlert*, September 21, 2004, available at **http://www.mrc.org/cyberalerts/2004/cyb20040921.asp#1** as of December 18, 2008

9. Howard Kurtz, "Dan Rather, In the Eye of the Storm," The *Washington Post*, October 3, 2004, p. D1

10. *Zogby International,* "Zogby Poll: Almost No Obama Voters Ace Election Test," November 18, 2008

11. *Reporters Without Borders,* "Press Freedom Index 2008," available at **http://www.rsf.org/article.php3?id_article=29034** as of December 21, 2008

12. *Reporters Without Borders,* "Xinhua: The World's Biggest Propaganda Agency," Report, October, 2005, available at **http://www.rsf.org/article.php3?id_article=15172** as of December 21, 2008

13. Ibid

14. The Constitution of the People's Republic of China, Chapter 2, Article 35

15. *Reporters Without Borders,* "Press Freedom in 2007," January 2, 2008

Chapter Three: History of Suppression

1. Rich Noyes, "Broadcast Blackout of Left's 'Fairness' Doctrine Push," *NewsBusters*, November 12, 2008

2. A. Thierer, "Why the fairness doctrine is anything but fair," *Heritage Foundation* Executive Memorandum #368, Oct. 29, 1993

3. "Fairness Doctrine," *The Museum of Broadcast Communications*, accessed online at http://www.museum.tv/archives/etv/F/htmlF/ fairnessdoct/fairnessdoct.htm.

4. Ibid

5. Ibid

6. Ibid

7. Ibid

8. U.S. Supreme Court, upholding the constitutionality of the Fairness Doctrine in *Red Lion Broadcasting Co. v. FCC*, 1969

9. A. Thierer, "Why the fairness doctrine is anything but fair," *Heritage Foundation*

10. Ibid

11. Ibid

12. The quotation is from Section III C of *Red Lion v. FCC* 395 U.S. 367 (1969)

13. *Telecommunications Research and Action Center v. FCC*, 801 F.2d 501

(D.C. Cir. 1986)

14. *Meredith Corp. v. FCC*, 809 F.2d 863, (D.C. Cir. 1987)

15. *Syracuse Peace Council v. FCC*, 867 F.2d 654 (D.C. Cir. 1989)

16. *FCC v. League of Women Voters*, 468 U.S. 364, Syllabus, Sect. (a)

17. Henry Geller, "Talk vs. Action at the FCC," *Regulation*, March/April 1983, p. 15

18. A. Thierer, "Why the fairness doctrine is anything but fair," *Heritage Foundation*

19. "Number of licensed radio stations grows," *Radio World Newspaper*, March 21, 2008, accessed online at **http://www.radioworld.com/pages/s.0100/t.12104.html**

20. Ibid

21. Thomas W. Hazlett, "The Fairness Doctrine and the First Amendment," *The Public Interest*, Summer 1989, p. 105

22. A. Thierer, "Why the fairness doctrine is anything but fair," *Heritage Foundation*

23. Ibid

24. Tony Snow, "Return of the Fairness Demon," The *Washington Times*, Sept. 5, 1993, p. B3

Chapter Four: Targeting Free Speech

1. Joseph Farah, "The day 'New Media' was born," *WorldNetDaily.com*, Oct. 31, 2007

2. Ibid

3. Ibid

4. Joseph Farah, "The coming First Amendment crackdown," *WorldNetDaily.com*, Oct. 30, 2008

5. Ibid

6. Ibid

7. Bob Cusack, "Schumer on Fox: Fairness Doctrine 'Fair and Balanced,'" *The Hill*, Nov. 4, 2008

8. Ibid

9. *Media Research Center*, "Petition to Stop the Fairness Doctrine," accessed online Nov. 13, 2008

10. John Eggerton, "Kerry wants fairness doctrine reimposed," *Broadcasting & Cable*, June 27, 2007

11. Joe Kovacs, "Rush Limbaugh: Regulate the 'Drive-by media,'" *WorldNetDaily.com*, July 11, 2007

12. Tim Graham, "Media Blog: Al Gore rips Reagan on Fairness Doctrine," *National Review Online*, May 30, 2007

13. Alexander Bolton, "Fairness Doctrine hammered 309-115,"

The Hill, June 27, 2007

14. Ibid

15. Ibid

16. Ibid

17. Ibid

18. Ibid

19. Joe Kovacs, "Rush Limbaugh: Regulate the 'Drive-by media,'" *WorldNetDaily.com*

20. Adam Thierer, "Return of the (Un)Fairness Doctrine: The Media Ownership Reform Act," *CATO Institute,* Issue #80, April 20, 2004

21. Ibid

22. Ibid

23. "State of the News Media 2008," *Project for Excellence in Journalism,* accessed online at **http://www.stateofthenewsmedia.org/2008/narrative_newspapers_audience.php?cat=2&media=4**

24. Ibid

25. Media Ownership Reform Act of 2005, Sect. 340, § (e)

26. Rep. Mike Pence, "Pence Unveils Bill to Prohibit Return of Fairness Doctrine for Talk Radio," June 27, 2007

27. Brett Joshpe, "Protecting Free Speech," *The American Spectator,*

December 18, 2008

28. Ibid

29. Ibid

30. Ibid

31. Ibid

32. Jo Mannies, "Report on Obama's "Truth Squad" Stirs Up Internet Frenzy," The *St. Louis Post-Dispatch*, September 30, 2008

33. "Reid Calls On Senators To Join In Condemning Limbaugh's Attack On Our Troops," *Democrats.Senate.gov Newsroom*, Oct. 1, 2007, accessed online at **http://democrats.senate.gov/newsroom/record. cfm?id=284592**

34. "Anatomy of a smear:'Phony soldiers' is a phony story," *Rushlimbaugh. com*, posted Sept. 28, 2007, accessed online at **http://www.rushlimbaugh. com/home/daily/site_092807/content/01125106.guest.html**

35. Ibid

36. Ibid

37. Joseph Farah, "The coming 1st Amendment crackdown," *WorldNetDaily.com*, Feb. 21, 2008

38. Joseph Farah, "The unfairness doctrine," *WorldNetDaily.com*, Jan. 25, 2007

39. "Hushing Rush and Hannity sounds great to Obama fans,"

WorldNetDaily.com, Oct. 27, 2008

40. Ibid

41. Ibid

42. Ibid

43. Paul Weyrich, "There should be no Fairness-Doctrine secret agenda," *Free Congress Foundation*, June 27, 2008

44. Ibid

45. Ibid

46. Ibid

47. Rep. Mike Pence (R-IN) "Send the Fairness Doctrine to the ash heap of broadcast history," *Human Events*

Chapter Five: The Incumbent Protection Act

1. George F. Will, "McCain-Feingold's Wealth of Hypocrisy," The *Washington Post*, November 22, 2007, page A37

2. Edward Crane, "Lamont's Victory Exposes the True Nature of Campaign Finance 'Reform,'" *CATO Institute*, August 9, 2006

3. Karl Rove, "McCain Couldn't Compete with Obama's Money," The *Wall Street Journal*, December 3, 2008

4. Cleta Mitchell, "Supreme Court Back Free Speech, Hits McCain-Feingold," *Human Events*, July 2, 2007

5. Bill Mears, "Supreme Court Allows Issue Ads in Federal Elections," *CNN.com*, June 25, 2007

6. Brian Anderson and Adam Thierer, *A Manifesto for Media Freedom*, Encounter Books, Copyright 2008, page 88

7. Scott Felsenthal, "Online Campaign Ads," *First Amendment Center*, April 26, 2007, available at **http://www.firstamendmentcenter.org/ speech/campaignfinance/topic.aspx?topic=online_campaign_ads** as of December 26, 2007

8. Brian Anderson and Adam Thierer, *A Manifesto for Media Freedom*, Encounter Books, Copyright 2008, page 89

9. Scott Felsenthal, "Online Campaign Ads," *First Amendment Center*, April 26, 2007, available at **http://www.firstamendmentcenter.org/ speech/campaignfinance/topic.aspx?topic=online_campaign_ads** as of December 26, 2007

10. Brian Anderson and Adam Thierer, *A Manifesto for Media Freedom*, Encounter Books, Copyright 2008, page 89

11. Brian Anderson and Adam Thierer, *A Manifesto for Media Freedom*, Encounter Books, Copyright 2008, page 90

12. Brian Anderson and Adam Thierer, *A Manifesto for Media Freedom*, Encounter Books, Copyright 2008, page 91

13. Bradley Smith, "Internet Regulation: The FEC Hits a Triple," *RedState.com*, available at **http://archive.redstate.com/ story/2006/3/25/113459/934** as of December 31, 2008

14. *GovTrack.us*, "House Vote On Passage: H.R. 1606 [109th]: Online

Freedom of Speech Act," available at **http://www.govtrack.us/ congress/vote.xpd?vote=h2005-559** as of January 1, 2008

15. *Rasmussen Reports*, "55% Say Media Bias Bigger Problem Than Campaign Cash," August 11, 2008

16. Hon. Clarence Thomas, *McCONNELL, UNITED STATES SENATOR, et al. v. FEDERAL ELECTION COMMISSION et al.*, December 10, 2003

Chapter Six: Sea of Voices

1. Brad O'Leary, "What Makes Mr. Cool Lose His Cool? Free Speech!" *News Blaze*, Oct. 27, 2008

2. Letter from Obama for America general counsel Robert F. Bauer

3. Ibid

4. Ibid

5. Adam Thierer, "The media cornucopia: We live in a Golden Age of information, but the Left would rein it in," *Chicago Sun-Times*, April 22, 2007

6. Figure provided by Jupiter Research, *Jupiter Media*, Nov. 22, 2005, accessed online at **http://www.jupitermedia.com/corporate/ releases/05.11.22-newjupresearch.html**

7. Figure provided by the *Heartland Institute*, Aug. 1, 2008, accessed online at **http://www.heartland.org/policybot/results.html?articleid=23527**

8. Thierer, "The media cornucopia: We live in a Golden Age of information, but the Left would rein it in," *Chicago Sun-Times*

9. Ibid

10. Heather Green, "With 15.5 million active blogs, new Technorati data shows that blogging growth may be peaking," *BusinessWeek*, April 25, 2007

11. Thierer, "The media cornucopia: We live in a Golden Age of information, but the Left would rein it in," *Chicago Sun-Times*

12. Adam Thierer, Grant Eskelsen, "Media Metrics: The True State of the Modern Media Marketplace," The *Progress Freedom Foundation* Special Report, Summer 2008, p. 9

13. Jack Shafer, "The Varieties of Media Bias, Part 1: Who Threw the First Punch in the Press Bias Brawl?" *Slate*, Feb. 5, 2003, http://slate.msn.com/id/2078200

14. Mary Stuckey, "Presidential Election and the Media," in Mark J. Rozell, ed., *Media Power, Media Politics* (Lanham, MD: Rowman & Littlefield, 2003), p. 159

15. Thierer, Eskelsen, "Media Metrics: The True State of the Modern Media Marketplace," The *Progress Freedom Foundation* Special Report, Summer 2008, p. 9

16. Ibid

17. Clay Shirky, *Here Comes Everybody: The Power of Organizing Without Organizations* (New York: The *Penguin Press*, 2008), p. 106

18. Thierer, Eskelsen, "Media Metrics: The True State of the Modern Media Marketplace," *The Progress*

19. *Freedom Foundation* Special Report, Summer 2008, p. 11

20. Thierer, Eskelsen, "Media Metrics: The True State of the Modern Media Marketplace," The *Progress Freedom Foundation* Special Report, Summer 2008, p. 16

21. As quoted by Thierer, Eskelsen, "Media Metrics: The True State of the Modern Media Marketplace," The *Progress Freedom Foundation* Special Report, Summer 2008, p. 16

22. Suzy Hansen, "Media O.D.," *Salon.com*, April 15, 2002, accessed online at http://dir.salon.com/story/books/int/2002/04/15/gitlin/

23. Adam Thierer, "The Media Cornucopia," *City Journal*, April 18, 2007

24. Ibid

Chapter Seven: Failure of Left-wing Talk

1. Jim Rutenberg, "Liberal radio is planned by rich group of Democrats," The *New York Times*, February 17, 2003

2. Ibid

3. "Free-fall Radio: Air America goes bankrupt," *The Smoking Gun*, accessed online at http://www.thesmokinggun.com/archive/1013062airamerica1.html

4. David Lombino, "Franken signed Air America's payment pact,"

New York Sun, Sept. 7, 2005

5. Ibid

6. Bill Niehuis, "The Failure of 'Progressive' Media," *PunditGuy.com*, April 26, 2006, accessed online at http://www.punditguy.com/2006/04/the_failure_of.html

7. Ibid

8. "The Top Talk Radio Audiences," *Talkers Magazine*, accessed online November 30, 2008 at http://www.talkers.com/main/index.php?option=com_content&task=view&id=17&Itemid=34

9. Joe Klein, "Bush's last days: The Lamest Duck," *Time*, November 26, 2008

10. Brian C. Anderson, "Why the Liberals Can't Keep Air America From Spiraling In," *Los Angeles Times*, April 18, 2005

11. Troy Appel, "Air America's failure show liberals have no place on talk-radio airwaves," The *Daily Northwestern*, April 16, 2004

Chapter Eight: Conservative Success on the Air

1. Jon Sinton, "Limbaugh is Right on the Fairness Doctrine," The *Wall Street Journal*, December 22, 2008

2. Daniel Henninger, "Rush to Victory: Why is Harry Reid acting like David Koresh? Because conservatives are winning," The *Wall Street Journal*, April 29, 2005

3. William G. Mayer, "Why talk radio is conservative," *Public Interest*, Summer 2004

4. Ibid

5. Ibid

6. Brian Fitzpatrick, "Unmasking the Myths Behind the Fairness Doctrine," *Media Research Center Special Report*, Executive Summary, 2008

7. Ibid

8. Mayer, "Why talk radio is conservative," *Public Interest*

9. Mayer, "Why talk radio is conservative," *Public Interest*

10. Brian C. Anderson, "Why the liberals can't keep Air America from spiraling in," *Los Angeles Times*, April 18, 2005

11. "Talk show listeners talk back on balance," *Business Wire*, July 9, 2003

12. Mayer, "Why talk radio is conservative," *Public Interest*

13. Anderson, "Why the liberals can't keep Air America from spiraling in," *Los Angeles Times*

14. Ibid

15. Mayer, "Why talk radio is conservative," *Public Interest*

16. Ibid

17. Ibid

18. Ibid

19. Ibid

20. Ibid

21. Marc Fisher, "Liberal talk radio already exists," *Slate.com*, February 21, 2003

22. Mayer, "Why talk radio is conservative," *Public Interest*

23. Ibid

24. Ibid

25. Sam Howe Verhovek, "Talk Radio Gets a Spirited New Voice from the Left," *The New York Times*, May 9, 1994

26. Mayer, "Why talk radio is conservative," *Public Interest*

27. Ibid

28. Ibid

Chapter Nine: Beyond Talk Radio

1. Jeff Poor, "FCC Commissioner: Return of Fairness Doctrine Could Control Web Content," *Business & Media Institute*, August 13, 2008

2. Ibid

3. Ibid

4. Ibid

5. Bill summary of the Communications Decency Act of 1995, Thomas W. Hazlett, David W. Sosa, "Chilling the Internet? Lessons from the FCC Regulation of Radio Broadcasting," *CATO Policy Analysis No. 270*, March 19, 1997

6. Ibid

7. "The Communications Act Defined," *CNN*, accessed online on December 4, 2008 at **http://www.cnn.com/US/9703/cda.scotus/ what.is.cda/index.html**

8. Bill summary of the Communications Decency Act of 1995, Thomas W. Hazlett, David W. Sosa, "Chilling the Internet? Lessons from the FCC Regulation of Radio Broadcasting," *CATO Policy Analysis*

9. Floyd Abrams, "Not under My First Amendment," *Cato's Letter, Vol. 3*, Number 4, Fall 2005

10. Cass Sunstein, *Republic.com 2.0*, August 2007

11. Joseph Farah, "When 'fairness' means 'censorship'," *WorldNetDaily.com*, November 20, 2008

12. Ibid

13. Adam Thierer, "A Fairness Doctrine for the Internet: Brought to you by NARAL and the Christian Coalition," *City Journal*, October 18, 2007

14. Brian C. Anderson, "Hands off the Net," *City Journal*, June 28, 2006

15. Thierer, "A Fairness Doctrine for the Internet: Brought to you by

NARAL and the Christian Coalition," *City Journal*

16. "The Verizon Warning," The *New York Times*, October 3, 2007

17. Thierer, "A Fairness Doctrine for the Internet: Brought to you by NARAL and the Christian Coalition," *City Journal*

18. Ibid

19. *Reporters Without Borders*, "The 15 Enemies of the Internet and Other Countries to Watch," November 17, 2005

Chapter Ten: Christian 'Hate Speech'

1. Emily Yoffe, "Was 'No King but Jesus' a Revolutionary War slogan?" *Slate.com*, January 18, 2001, accessed online at **http://www.slate.com/id/1006902/**

2. Joseph Farah, "Repeal the Johnson Amendment," *WorldNetDaily.com*, February 25, 2008

3. Joshua Patty, "U.S. History: Toleration in South," *AllExperts.com*, September 4, 2006

4. Farah, "Repeal the Johnson Amendment," *WorldNetDaily.com*

5. Internal Revenue Service code, Rev. Rul. 86-95, IRS Revenue Ruling, published Aug. 11, 1986, accessed online at **http://www.campaignlegalcenter.org/attachments/1189.pdf**

6. Farah, "Repeal the Johnson Amendment," *WorldNetDaily.com*

7. Ibid

8. IRS correspondence to Rev. Wiley Drake, dated May 12, 2008, accessed online at http://www.ocregister.com/newsimages/news/2008/05/irs_comboletter_.pdf

9. Farah, "Repeal the Johnson Amendment," *WorldNetDaily.com*

10. Jeff White, "Christian Radio Under Attack by FCC," *ChristianWebsite.com*, July 17, 2008, accessed online at http://www.christianwebsite.com/christian-radio-under-attack-by-fcc/

11. Larry West, "For Gods Sake: Religious Organizations Preach Environmental Stewardship," *About.com*, accessed December 9, 2008

12. V. Klaus, "Blue Planet in Green Shackles," *Competitive Enterprise Institute*, 2007

13. Andrea S. Lafferty, "Liberals seek to kill conservative talk radio as 'hate speech,'" *Traditional Values Coalition* Web site on December 9, 2008 at http://www.traditionalvalues.org/modules.php?sid=3123

14. Jay Sekulow, "Defending the Airwaves," The *American Center for Law and Justice*, February 9, 2007, available at http://www.aclj.org/TrialNotebook/Read.aspx?id=449 as of December 24, 2008

15. Ibid

16. Lafferty, "Liberals seek to kill conservative talk radio as 'hate speech,'" *Traditional Values Coalition* Web site

17. Dr. Frank Wright, "Statutory Reimposition of the 'Fairness Doctrine' Would be Unconstitutional," *National Religious Broadcasters*, NRB White Paper, July 2007

18. Ibid

19. Art Moore, "Bible Verses Regarded as Hate Literature," *WorldNetDaily.com*, February 18, 2003

20. Brett Joshpe, "Protecting Free Speech," The *American Spectator*, December 18, 2008

21. *WorldNetDaily.com*, "Swedish Minister Acquitted of Hate Speech Charges," November 29, 2005

22. The *Christian Institute*, "Churchman 'Guilty' Under Aussie Hate Speech Law for Criticising Islam Visits UK," News Release, February 2, 2005

Chapter Eleven: What Congress Will Attempt to Do

1. *CATO Handbook for Congress*, Chapter 20, CATO Institute, accessed online at **http://www.cato.org/pubs/handbook/hb105-20.html**, December 11, 2008

2. Ibid

3. Ibid

4. Ibid

5. Ibid

6. "Creative Arts, Media and Free Speech Groups Join ACLU In Urging Supreme Court To Reject FCC Censorship," *American Civil Liberties Union* press release, August 7, 2008

7. *CATO Handbook for Congress*, Chapter 20, CATO Institute

8. Ibid

9. Ibid

10. Marsha West, "NBC Squashes Bob the Tomato's Free Speech," *NewswithViews.com*, October 6, 2006

11. Rev. Jerry Falwell, "ABC Bleeps Out 'Jesus,'" *WorldNetDaily.com*, June 1, 2002

12. James L. Gattuso, "Fairness Doctrine R.I.P.," *National Review Online*, July 5, 2007

13. Ibid

14. Ibid

15. Ibid

16. Bobby Eberle, "Coalition stand strong against the 'Fairness Doctrine,'" *GOPUSA.com*, November 14, 2007

Chapter Twelve: What the FCC Could Do

1. "Obama to appoint talk radio's executioner?" *WorldNetDaily.com*, November 8, 2008.

2. Ibid

3. "Obama names FCC transition team," *CNET*, November 14, 2008

4. Stephen Labaton, "Obama to Select Genachowski to Lead FCC," The *New York Times*, January 13, 2009

5. The Office of the President-Elect, "Agenda, Technology," available at **http://change.gov/agenda/technology_agenda/**

6. Matt Cover, "Acting FCC Chair Sees Government Role in Pushing 'Media Diversity,'" *CNSNews.com*, February 12, 2009

7. Ibid

8. Ibid

9. Jim Abrams, "FCC Chair: Fairness Doctrine not needed," The *Associated Press*, July 26, 2007

10. Ibid

11. "A Manifesto for Freedom," The *Progress & Freedom Foundation* news release, October 2, 2008

12. Ibid

13. "About the Federal Communications Commission," *FCC* Web site, accessed December 15, 2008 at **http://www.fcc.gov/aboutus.html**

Chapter Fourteen: Meet the Guardians of Free Speech

1. George Will, "Reactionary Liberals Assault the Media," *Townhall.com*, December 7, 2008

2. Tony Blankley, "Liberals Leave the Watchtowers of Freedom," *Townhall.com*, December 10, 2008

3. William Rusher, "Beware of the 'Fairness Doctrine,'" *Townhall.com*, November 24, 2008

4. Michael Barone, "The Coming Obama Thugocracy," *National Review*, October 11, 2008

5. David Limbaugh, "The Un-Fairness Doctrine: Unevening the Playing Field, by Law," *Townhall.com*, January 19, 2007

6. Paul Greenberg, "The Unfairness Doctrine," *The Washington Times*, October 18, 2008

7. John Fund, "Fairness is Foul," The *Wall Street Journal*, October 29, 2007

8. Joseph Farah, "Misunderstanding the 'Fairness Doctrine,'" *WorldNetDaily.com*, January 10, 2009

9. Paul Weyrich, "Illusion or Actuality? Many Prominent Media Figures and Democrats Oppose Fairness Doctrine Re-imposition," *Townhall.com*, October 22, 2008

About the Author

Brad O'Leary serves as president of ATI-News, an online magazine and information Website that provides links to more than 750 English newspapers and magazines worldwide. He is also publisher of The O'Leary Report (www.olearyreport.com).

O'Leary is also Chairman of the Board of PM Direct Marketing, one of the country's leading Perception Management firms representing numerous U.S. senators, corporations and associations. He is also former president of the American Association of Political Consultants.

From 1993 to 1997, Brad O'Leary hosted a talk show program on NBC Westwood One that boasted two million listeners a day. He was also a cover story and feature writer for *USA Today Weekend Magazine* with 100 million weekly readers.

O'Leary is the author of twelve books, including:

The Audacity of Deceit: Barack Obama's War on American Values

Audacity sat atop Amazon's election bestseller list and was ranked #1 in its "executive branch" category and #2 in its "current events" category.

According to *Human Events*: "Brad O'Leary goes beyond the messianic hype and examines the real Obama record, along with his proposals on the issues that are at the forefront... Read *The Audacity of Deceit* carefully, and use it to try to awaken your friends and coworkers to the threat this man poses to America."

The *Examiner's* Michelle Kerns wrote about Audacity: "You've got to hand it to author Brad O'Leary: the man has got chutzpah... *The Audacity of Deceit's* release promises to have the same effect on the

2008 presidential campaign as throwing a gasoline-soaked torch into a warehouse of fireworks – loud, spectacular, and memorable."

Presidential Follies

Human Events called *Follies* "as one-sided and impertinent as all getout, and yet it's also acute, knowing and percipient, not to mention wonderfully readable."

U.S. Senator Phil Gramm remarked: "Brad O'Leary is one of the most creative and experienced observers on the contemporary political scene."

According to Bill Murchison of the *Dallas Morning News*, "O'Leary entertains, educates and occasionally infuriates, all between the same set of covers."

Are You a Conservative or a Liberal?

According to *Roll Call*, "This...paperback is a fun test to show folks where they stand on the political spectrum."

Rush Limbaugh said, "I took the test and [O'Leary] got it right."

Triangle of Death

Publisher's Weekly said *Triangle*, which is a compelling recount of the fateful events that led to the death of President John F. Kennedy, put forth a "colorful theory, implicating a French heroin syndicate, the U.S. mob and the South Vietnamese government."

O'Leary is also the executive producer or producer of eleven television series and twenty-seven television specials, including these award-winning programs:

Ronald Reagan: An American President

EGO Magazine called it: "A gloriously comprehensive collection of the most memorable events in Reagan's life and presidency...a must have for any serious fan of the Gipper."

The Planet is Alive (a documentary chronicling the life of Pope John Paul II)

The *L.A. Herald Examiner* called it "pure magic."
The *St. Louis Review* said it is "spellbinding."
Variety calls it "extraordinary and compelling."